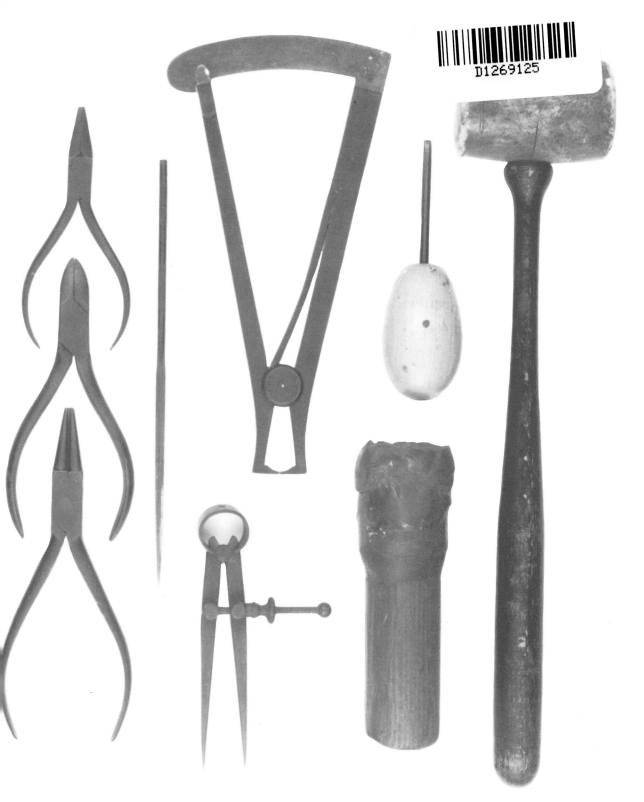

Jewellery tools loaned by Richard Smith

Twentieth Century British Jewellery

also by Peter Hinks

NINETEENTH CENTURY JEWELLERY

Twentieth Century British Jewellery

1900–1980

PETER HINKS

faber and faber LONDON · BOSTON

First published in 1983
by Faber and Faber Limited
3 Queen Square London WC1N 3AU
Printed in Great Britain by
BAS Printers Ltd
Over Wallop Hampshire

British Library Cataloguing in Publication Data

Hinks, Peter
Twentieth century British jewellery
1. Jewellery, British—History
I. Title
739.27'0941   NK7343

ISBN 0–571–10801–6

Library of Congress Cataloging in Publication Data

Hinks, Peter
Twentieth century British jewellery, 1900–1980
1. Jewelry—Great Britain—History—20th century
I. Title
NK7343.H56 1983   739.27'0941   83–5520

ISBN 0–571–10801–6

Contents

All pieces illustrated are reproduced life-size unless otherwise indicated

Colour Plates

Acknowledgements

The author is greatly indebted to

DE BEERS CONSOLIDATED MINES LTD
JOHNSON MATTHEY
THE PLATINUM SHOP (AYRTON METALS LTD)
THE SOCIETY OF JEWELLERY HISTORIANS
SOTHEBY'S
THE WORSHIPFUL COMPANY OF GOLDSMITHS

for the generous financial support they have given which has made possible a substantial increase in the number of colour plates in the book.

He would also like to thank Aspect, Brian Beaumont Nesbitt, Christies, Dunhill, Electrum Gallery, Prudence Glynn, Graus Antiques, Nick Harris, Elsa Hinks, Leah Hinks, Louis Kaplan, Mary Keays, Mrs L. Lloyd, Nonesuch Antiques, The Platinum Shop (Ayrton Metals Ltd), Alex Rhodes, Sotheby's, The Victoria and Albert Museum, Young Stephen and The Worshipful Company of Goldsmiths for allowing him to reproduce illustrations of jewels in their care; and Clare Matthews for her help in preparing the manuscript.

To the Worshipful Company of Goldsmiths

Introduction

Much has happened since this book was begun: new styles and exciting and unfamiliar materials have emerged; traditional ideas of what jewellery is for and the reasons for making it in the first place have been challenged. All this has kept the book, and the last chapter in particular, in a ferment of re-examination and revision. Now at the start of the eighties and from the precarious vantage point of yet another world depression, it is possible to discern how the two craft revivals relate to the present century and to the one which preceded it.

The art jeweller was a child of the late nineteenth-century aesthetic movement, set apart, as his patrons thought, from the rough and tumble of the common trade— and without doubt men like the Giulianos did bring a more than ordinary talent to their work. But the precedent was a dangerous one and the thinking behind it eventually brought about in the Arts and Crafts movement a kind of alternative culture which consciously strove to be separate and aloof from establishment fashion, society and economics. Since the eighteen-nineties there have been two distinct streams of creativity, represented on the one hand by the work of the 'craftsman jeweller', as we like to call him today, and on the other by the commercial products of trade and industry. One of the aims of this book is to chart the course of these movements through the century so far.

The distinctions between them are fraught with paradox and seem to have little to do with either 'art' or 'craft'. The making of a fine piece of diamond jewellery in the workshops of one of the great commercial houses calls for hand craftsmanship of the very highest order and leaves one wondering whether the term 'craftsman jeweller' has much relevance in the sense in which we use it.

Most craftsman jewellers are art-school graduates and yet our government art colleges were founded with the avowed intention of training designers for industry. Their creations may be stunningly beautiful, technically brilliant or exuberantly impracticable, but they hardly ever reach the commercial workshops where they would do most good. The principal difference between the jewellers of the craft revival and those of the orthodox trade lies in their respective attitudes, and perhaps

Introduction

the only thing they have in common is the suspicion and intolerance with which one side regards the other.

Baffling and exasperating although the schism may be, it has contributed to the dazzling variety of jewellery made in this country during the present century, from the frothy saw-pierced platinum and pavé diamonds of the *belle époque* to the luminous acrylic and iridescent titanium of the space-age eighties. It is a diversity which reflects the helter-skelter of social and technical change we have lived through since 1900.

To a craft whose tools, methods and materials had altered little since the middle ages, the twentieth century has brought many changes, especially recently, and platinum, anodized aluminium and the refractory metals have made possible many jewels which could never have existed before. Twentieth-century Britain not only has much to gratify the jewellery collector's magpie soul, but it gives him the chance of assuming the lofty and creative role of the patron by commissioning a jewel from a living craftsman.

At its most practical level this book should help the collector to identify his acquisitions and perhaps suggest some paths for him to follow. In the face of such a wealth of material the author has been obliged to be selective: to take any other approach would have resulted in a work which would have been difficult to read and almost impossible to carry. Occasionally jewels are mentioned which either originated abroad or before 1900 and which may therefore seem on the face of it to be outside our terms of reference. That is because they were either such a vital part of British fashion or such a seminal influence upon it that it was impossible to ignore them.

For the most part the jewels and jewellers described in these pages are those which the collector is most likely to come across, those which typify a style or trend and those which are exceptionally curious or beautiful. The problem has not been so much what to put in as what to leave out. The author has tried to be objective in both choice and emphasis, but there may be occasions where admiration and enthusiasm have got the better of him. For this he makes no apology.

1 · The Edwardian Period—1900 to 1914

In 1900 Great Britain was at war with the Boers. It was a gloomy start to the new century. Casualties were shockingly heavy and society was overshadowed by events in Africa. Balls and parties were all too often cancelled and more and more women were to be seen in mourning. Soldier's khaki was briefly fashionable, but the colour of the year 1900 was undoubtedly black, and on black nothing looks better than diamonds. Diamonds were considered perfectly proper even in deep mourning for a near relative and the more of them the better.

Late Victorian mourning was a splendid affair and when Alexandra, then Princess of Wales and a simple dresser by inclination, appeared at a masque in aid of the widows and orphans of the household troops it was in the awesome full dress of Imperial sympathy—black mousseline-de-soie encrusted with jet, hair transfixed with a jewelled arrow and crested with trembling egret plumes, and of course diamonds, big diamond brilliants cascading from throat to waist in chokers, sautoirs and rivières.

The South African war had little direct effect on designs however. Gentlemen might wear a pair of gold and platinum cufflinks representing a Lee Metford rifle cartridge and a shrapnel shell (price £2 15s) and a shilling or so would buy a charm with the portraits of Generals Roberts and Buller or miniature effigies of 'The Soldiers of the Queen' to hang on bracelet or watch-chain. The war was responsible for a multitude of Kruger gold coins being made up into pendants, bracelets and watch-chain charms. Frank Isherwood describes the wedding plans of a brother officer: 'Six bridesmaids in Empire dresses and bouquets and long blue wands. Each of the Bridesmaids is to have a Kruger half sovereign dangling on a curb Bracelet. The men who walk with them are to have a pin with half a merrythought[1] on it. The other half of the merrythought is to be presented by the man to what this fellow calls "his best girl". It all sounds most vulgar and sykesy I thought.'[2]

1. Wishbone—author's note.
2. Christopher Isherwood, *Kathleen and Frank*, 1971.

The Edwardian Period—1900 to 1914

TRANSITION—LATE VICTORIAN TO EDWARDIAN

The jewellers' catalogues of 1900 were packed with designs which had recurred year after year for the previous two decades. Diamond stars, crescents and targets were as popular as ever. Stars generally came in sets of five which could be worn either singly as brooches and pendants or put together into a tiara or necklace at will. Crescent brooches were usually provided with a pronged device of silver gilt which allowed them to be worn in the hair. Diamond pendants in the form of a Maltese cross were a revival from the eighteen-thirties, and the posies of diamond roses, marguerites, daisies and other flowers of the English garden and wayside had an even longer pedigree which went right back to the eighteenth century.

In the mercurial world of fashion conservatism like this is seldom without good reason. These styles were not only good looking and versatile, but often robust and easy to wear too, and they combined the simplicity of traditional good taste with the opulence and dignity that a Victorian grand occasion demanded.

Victorian and Edwardian styles overlapped quite appreciably: these Victorian designs persisted until after 1905 and by the same token many jewels of the nineties were Edwardian rather than Victorian in spirit. The aigrette, a jewelled plume, usually of the snowy hair-like plumage of the egret, though it first appeared in the nineties, really came into its own as a finishing touch to Poiret's harem styles in 1910 and was still the height of fashion in the twenties (Plate 1).

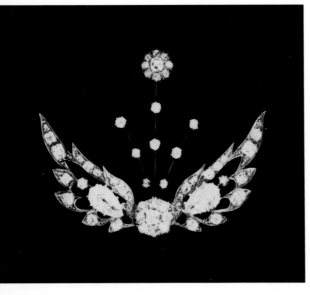

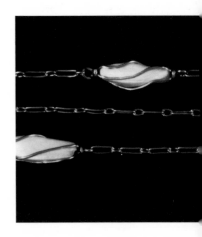

1. *A diamond* AIGRETTE *to be worn with an egret plume*

14

The sautoir, or muff-chain, was a simple continuous chain which could be worn in a number of different ways. When it was invented just after the French Revolution it was worn *en sautoir* or bandolier fashion across the shoulders, but women soon devised other ways of wearing this simple ornament. It is this versatility which has called the sautoir back into fashion more than once since that time. It could be worn doubled or trebled around the neck, hitched up in festoons or tucked into a belt, and the tight pocketless skirts of the early nineteen-hundreds made them particularly useful for holding a small purse, a watch or a lorgnette.

Gold chains were made in many 'fancy' patterns, each of which had a more or less appropriate trade name: fetter, secret link, alma, Spanish tie—Prince of Wales chain was a spiral pattern resembling a supple cord. Other chains of the more orthodox trace-link or wheat patterns were given an excitingly barbaric appearance by being interrupted every few inches by nuggets of uncut turquoise matrix or Mississippi mussel-pearls with the wrinkled silvery gleam of whitebait, each gem imprisoned in a cage-like setting of gold wire (Plate 2). A variation on this and perhaps the prettiest of all was a slim trace-chain with batons of enamel and small sea-pearls every inch or so (Plate 3). Others were set with multitudinous coloured stones from the river gravels of Ceylon—blue sapphires which turned to a fashionable lilac tint at night, spinels of inky blue or strawberry red, rich-brown hessonite garnets and golden zircons. These gems were spectacle-set—held by a light rim of gold around the girdle. Diamonds sometimes received the same treatment (Plate 4) and Alexandra herself was often seen in a superb chain set with large brilliants.

Not all sautoirs were so preciously fashioned however, and in 1901 many were simply strung from onyx, glass or coral beads. Since a sautoir could be worn two or even three times round the neck it could be of almost any size. Gaby Deslys, the

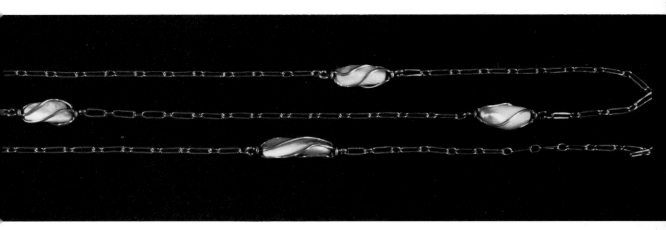

2. A SAUTOIR *of Mississippi pearls in cage settings*

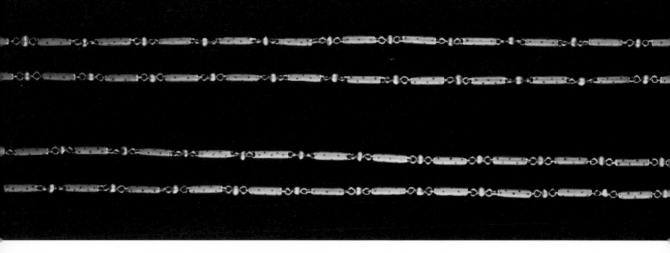

3. A SAUTOIR *of pink enamel and pearls*

actress, had one of pearl given to her by the King of Portugal. A probably apocryphal story tells how in a violent quarrel with the king on board ship she tore the pearls from her body and flung them over the side. Later the repentant monarch sent her an identical string although Gaby, it appears, chose not to mar the tenderness of the reconciliation by telling the king that the pearls which she had thrown into the sea had been a cheap imitation replica.[3]

Chokers, or dog collars, also came in during the declining years of the nineteenth century and remained until the First World War. The fashion was started by Alexandra who wore a choker to hide a small scar on her throat, and although it was an uncomfortable jewel she was copied by fashionable women everywhere. The classic design was of rows of small pearls kept parallel by panels of diamond openwork.

It is not easy to decide the exact point at which a jewel becomes a dress accessory and perhaps it does not very much matter. Either way, the buckles of the late Victorian and Edwardian era are not easy to ignore, especially when scores of them could be scattered over a single outfit and when the best of them could be set with hundreds of pounds worth of diamonds. The belts worn were so wide that in 1906 they had to be boned like a corset and buckles were correspondingly large. They could be worn either at the front or the back of the waist or even simultaneously in both places. Seldom was their purpose much more than decorative: the wrap-over

3. John Culme.

front of a bodice could be secured with a deep narrow buckle, or a hundred or more of them could be strewn over a smart visiting-dress. Buckles could be worn in the hair, either with a turban-like twist of tulle, or three of them together on a ribbon. In 1901 they had some desultory competition from lacings tipped with neat grelots or points but the style did not catch on and by next season the buckle was back without ever having been away.

Quite often one comes across a buckle neatly boxed with a set of six buttons: most of these date from around 1905 when decorative buttons were all the rage—not just for their traditional use of fastening a garment, but for trimming an Empire corsage, a skirt or a bolero. Most of these little suites were of silver, either enamelled, or with a relief decoration in art nouveau or rococo style.

The death of the queen in 1901 plunged society even deeper into mourning and this sombre event was commemorated in jewels just as the diamond jubilee had been celebrated a few years earlier. A black enamel V entwined with the date 1901 traced out in pearls formed a brooch, and a gold pendant carried a portrait of the late queen and the inscription in black 'Victoria R.I. obit Jan 22 1901'.

HIGH EDWARDIAN

When Albert Edward Prince of Wales was crowned Edward King and Emperor in 1902 the brooding shadow of the widowed queen was banished from fashionable

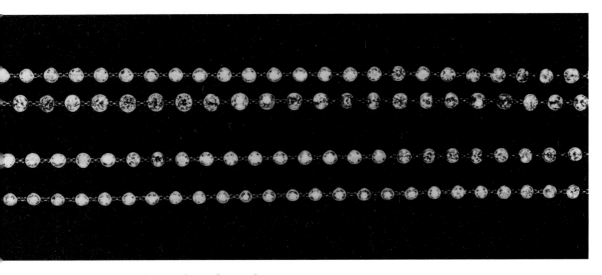

4. A SAUTOIR *of spectacle-set diamonds*

London. He seemed to embody in himself the paradoxical spirit of Edwardian life, its oddly felicitous blend of exuberance and restraint, fantasy and formality, gaiety and sense of style.

The king was a dandy, and however eccentric, his clothes were carefully chosen and meticulously worn: he successfully introduced the white topper for racing, tried to bring back knee breeches for evening wear and was even to be seen with his trousers carefully pressed sideways along the seams. It was not that he was out to defy and confound the old conventions but rather to introduce new ones of his own. At dinner, while Prince of Wales, he was heard to remark to a lady, 'The Princess has taken the trouble to wear a tiara—why haven't you?'[4] The snakes and ladders of fashionable life had to be played according to the rules, if only for the pleasure of seeing them broken with audacity and style.

At the opening of parliament in 1903 the peeresses wore tiaras instead of coronets and they wore them with a difference; not with the customary military precision, squarely on the head, but with a certain flair. Nothing is more unkind to an ageing complexion than a tiara crammed upon the brow like a crown of thorns. The peeresses of 1903 wore them perched impudently on the back of the head supported by a coil of hair or with the hair dressed low like a coronet. With great good sense the hair was used, it seems, to temper and soften the chilling effect of so many diamonds worn in the daytime.

The very latest fashion in tiaras sprouted two large diamonds on slender quivering antennae. Outlandish fashions seldom last long and no such tiaras are known to be in existence today. Most of them must long since have had the big stones clipped off and converted into earrings. However, this idea, which is so much in the fey art nouveau idiom, survived in other guises. The large hatpins originally intended to anchor vast millinery to the head were now worn sticking out on either side of a small, close-fitting hat. Diamond hatpins were even sold with prongs of tortoiseshell which could be screwed on instead of the pin, allowing them to be worn in the evening in the same fashion.

Many were the ways in which an imaginative woman could make the most of her hair: Lady Beatrice Pole Carew preferred a broad bandeau of diamonds to a tiara some years before this particular fashion took a firm hold, and Lady Feo Stuart wore a fillet of coloured tulle caught down with diamond slides. The queen herself was responsible for the popularity of the Imperial Russian tiara. A superbly simple design, which is said to have been inspired by the gala head-dress of a Russian peasant girl, the Imperial Russian tiara encircled the head with a blazing palisade of diamonds.

4. Phillip Magnus, *King Edward the Seventh*, London 1964.

18

Many actually were Russian and of some age, but the style is also known to have been copied by London jewellers.

Queen Alexandra, besides being the most beautiful queen in Europe, was a woman of great charm and innate simplicity. Before her marriage she had been accustomed to making her own clothes, and even as queen she preferred to dispense with jewellery altogether in the daytime and to wear only a single rose. Naturally the society women of the day looked to her for an example and they too wore roses, only the petals were of dainty pink enamel about a single-diamond centre. Incidentally, this fashion was a great success and other flowers were copied in this way, pansies, primroses and even water-lilies (Plate 5). Violets with velvet petals edged with diamonds were an interesting variation on the same theme.

Most fashionable Edwardian women wore a lot of jewellery and in 1909 it was noticed that even the queen was wearing more jewellery in the daytime. It was not at all uncommon for a lady to take tea with a bracelet on each wrist and at least one ring on every finger. Rings could be large too, sometimes occupying the lower joint of the finger from knuckle to knuckle (Plate 6). The most popular of these designs had an oval or boat-shaped cluster of brilliants or a pavé-set oblong or hexagonal plaque for a bezel. Rings of this size were rarely seen on the Victorian woman and like so many other jewels of the period hark back to Georgian times.

Many rings were of Victorian origin, though, and some of them like the cross-over and the half-hoop are still with us today. The multiple-hoop ring, although reputedly of Russian origin, was very much in Edwardian taste and lasted at least until 1910. It was made from several slender rose-diamond-fronted gold hoops, four or more of them, each set at intervals with a different gem—rubies, sapphires, pearls, green garnets and so on—and united at the back with a band of gold (Plate 7).

5. (left) *A gold, enamel and diamond water-lily* BROOCH
6. (centre) *A turquoise and rose-diamond* RING *with art nouveau scrollwork*
7. (right) *A multi-hoop* RING *set with rose diamonds and coloured stones*

*8. A diamond and opal
gadfly* BROOCH

Brooches, too, were also worn several at a time. A photograph of Belle Ellmore shows her wearing three at a low horizontal décolletage, a cluster, a coronet and a bar, selected with her habitual lack of taste. Perhaps it was one of these brooches which led to the downfall of her unfortunate husband Dr Ernest Crippen, for his mistress Ethel le Neve was seen wearing one of the late Belle's brooches at a charity ball soon after the murder. Marie Lloyd was the first to notice it, for she had a good eye for jewellery and the few pieces she owned were said to have been of the highest quality.

Fashions in 1907 made these brooches a necessity for anchoring the masses of falling lace on the corsage. At Ascot in 1909 it was noticed that the queen wore several brooches among the chiffon and lace trimmings of her gown. In ancient times brooches were nearly always functional, designed to fasten clothes together before buttons were invented. Similarly in the late nineteenth century brooches were devised to fasten the lace fichu. The bar brooch was designed with this in mind; it was a horizontal bar, usually with a simple decoration at the centre and ends. Edwardian versions were set with a single row of calibré-cut coloured stones or diamond brilliants or were of plain gold with a stone collet set at the centre in a ring of enamel. Blouse pins were sold in sets of four; small gold safety pins with a flying swallow, or perhaps a tiny turquoise at their centres, all contained in a little lizard skin wallet. Butterfly, dragonfly and bee brooches had been popular for some time (Colour

9. A pair of gold, amethyst and diamond lace PINS

10. A diamond and pearl bow BROOCH

Plates II and IIIc); even the noxious gadfly was a familiar subject (Plate 8) and gold and moonstone scorpions were common. A particularly charming design had two diminutive brooches—ribbon bows, moths, tortoises, swallows, even a spider and a fly—connected by a short chain (Plate 9).

When brooches were so closely related to the clothing they were worn with it is not surprising that they took on something of its character. Ribbon and drape designs abounded—sometimes even a bow of black velvet was held in a light diamond openwork mount to allow it to be worn as a brooch. Vesta Tilley, the music-hall male impersonator popularized cufflinks made from black-velvet ribbon bows. The story goes that her maid forgot her cufflinks and she improvized a pair from a hair ribbon.

Diamond brooches in the form of a ribbon bow have recurred time and time again since they were invented in the late seventeenth century (Plate 10). Some Edwardian designs are characterized by their own distinctive brand of careless formality and are tied in a most elegantly lopsided fashion. Others are almost puritanical in their neatness. They may be as big as a hand or no larger than a thumbnail.

The Juliet brooch was introduced by the Association of Diamond Merchants in 1906. It consisted of a barbed gold pin headed by a Mississippi pearl; a chain from the head was ringed over the exposed point to secure it and finished with a second pearl. It was also made in amethyst, peridot and topaz and it sold for ten and sixpence.

Pendant designs were often informal and unassuming, pared down to their barest essentials. The Edna May, for example, named after the lovely American actress, was nothing more than a simply set diamond brilliant or cluster hanging from a smaller stone by a slender undecorated link (Plate 11), whilst in the la Vallière the pendent

11. *A diamond Edna May* PENDANT

stone was pear-shaped. In others two pendants hang side by side from links of unequal length. Again the idea was not new, for necklaces with unequal drops were popular in the eighteen-thirties (Plates 12, 13, Colour Plate IIIb).

NOVELTY JEWELS

The light-hearted spirit of the age, although it occasionally lapsed into triviality, seldom manifested itself in the sort of vulgarity in which the Victorians revelled. Many novelty jewels were made and worn which, although almost embarrassingly 'cute' at times, do have a certain innocent charm. Some, like the bracelets inscribed with the entreaty 'Dinna Forget', or the charms representing a heart held between the poles of a magnet, were gages of love. Others like the tiepins representing a game

12. *A diamond* NÉGLIGÉ

13. *A ruby and diamond* NÉGLIGÉ *of a rather more elaborate design than is usual*

of diabolo (a craze in 1903), the charm like a coronation chair, the Easter egg pomanders and lockets or the misteltoe brooches were topical or at least seasonal in motivation.

There were lucky charms without number: pigs (Plate 15), beans, shamrocks, clover leaves and horseshoes (Colour Plate IIIh) in every kind of material from 18-carat gold and enamel or turquoise to golden-green Connemara marble and silver.

There were jewels also which reflected the wearer's own special hobby or preoccupation: those brooches in the form of an early motor car (Plate 14), a steering wheel or a hooter are a nostalgic reminder of the days when motoring was

14. *A gold, green-enamel and rose-diamond motor-car* BROOCH

23

15. *A diamond alley-cat* BROOCH *and a lucky-pig* CHARM

not an unavoidable necessity but a sport. Ladies even wore a special pin to keep their veiled hats on—it was like a big safety pin with a jewelled ball at each end. There were bracelets like an automobile drive-chain, and charms described as motor mascots which represent policemen, tigers, alley cats (Plate 15), dogs and so on—seeing them, one can almost hear the ecstatic 'poop poop' of the motormanic Mr Toad.

The king's enthusiasm for sailing must have been partly responsible for the boom in yachting jewellery: port and starboard navigation lights, signal flags and burgees in enamel or tinted crystal (Plate 16), watch-chain pendants set with a miniature compass. Benzie of Cowes made a speciality of this sort of thing.

Later on, when manned flight became a reality, 'aeronautical jewellery' was introduced. In 1909 pendants were made representing an aeroplane or a dirigible, its gas envelope convincingly imitated by a suitably shaped Mississippi pearl. Perhaps it

16. *A* BRACELET *of tinted crystal signal-flags with semaphore and morse code engraved on the pendent tablet*

17. A gold and pearl rabbit and turnip BROOCH *advertised by the Goldsmiths' and Silversmiths' Company in 1902*

would not be too far-fetched to speculate upon whether those jewels designed as diamond wings were inspired by the dream of flight (Colour Plate IIIb). Certainly these designs were popular right until the First World War. The successful production of Rostand's comedy *Chanticleer* not only gave this fashion an extra fillip, but was directly responsible for those tiepins and brooches of farmyard roosters in diamonds and enamel.

Many novelties seem to have had no excuse other than their originality: a gold and pearl winkle charm; a rabbit and turnip brooch (Plate 17); a frog in a frying pan; and those exquisite brooches in which a diamond monkey climbs a branch hauling behind it a watch on a long chain—unfortunately the monkey has long since been parted from the watch in most cases. Monkeys seem to have been great favourites with the Edwardians and occur time and again in literature and the decorative arts into the twenties (Colour Plate IIIi).

New Zealand tikis, the wide-eyed little figures carved by the Maoris from their native greenstone, had a brief hour of popularity after Leopold de Rothschild was given one just before his horse won the Derby in 1904.[5] Of course there were the inevitable silly-season ephemera. Living jewels made a comeback—chameleons tethered to a bracelet so that they could roam over their owner's hand and wrist. The fashion, if it could be called such, lasted no longer than it did when it first came in some forty years before, and there is no evidence to show that it even survived the summer of 1903.[6]

Little dogs seem to have been a sort of fashion accessory like a lorgnette or a muff. Late Edwardian fashion plates of a smart woman out walking usually show her towing a little ball of fluff, like a yacht under full sail with its diminutive dinghy. The craze manifested itself not only in the brooches representing the owner's favourite

5. *Illustrated London News*, 30 July 1904.
6. *Illustrated London News*, 22 August 1903.

breed, but in the jewelled bangles and pendants designed to be worn by the animal itself. Eleanor Glynn's sensational heroine of *Three Weeks* gives a gold collar to Paul Verdayne for his dog Pike.[7]

GEMS AND THEIR CUTTING

Heliotrope was Alexandra's favourite colour and mauves and purples in umpteen different shades and under many names became the fashion colours of the day. She wore a magnificent parure of amethysts when occasion demanded, setting a fashion for the deep-purple stones that lasted for as long as she was queen.

The king's favourite stone was said to be the leek-green peridot, a predilection probably wished upon him when he was still Prince of Wales. Prices rose as jewellers competed with one another for stocks. The finest stones came from the island of St John in the Red Sea and the Goldsmiths' and Silversmiths' Company successfully negotiated a mining concession with the Khedive of Egypt in 1904. The delicious muted green of the peridot was perfect for the fashionable Louis Quinze designs of the time—on the latticed background of a rococo cartouche, for example, or as a pendant, hanging freely within a garland of diamond flowers.

Turquoises were thought to be lucky and they were probably the most popular of all the coloured stones. No woman with any pretensions to style would have been without her 'bit of blue' as it was called and turquoises were in great demand for setting in charms and *porte-bonheurs*.

Amethyst and peridots remained firm favourites for many years, and so did New Mine sapphires. The 'new mine' was situated in Yogo Gulch, Montana, and the stones it yielded had a distinctive steely brilliance. Although rarely of any size, they had the great advantage of holding their colour in artificial light and not turning black like an Australian stone, or purple like many of those from Ceylon.

Other fashions in gems came and went: green tourmaline in 1903; pink Kunzites and tangerine Mexican fire opals in 1904, yellow sapphires in 1908 (Colour Plate IVd), Australian opals in 1909 (Colour Plate IVe). The small demantoid garnet from Siberia is similar to the peridot in colour, but rivals the diamond in fire and lustre, qualities which the jeweller used cleverly to suggest the brilliance of a reptile or an insect. Streeter of Bond Street specialized in the more recherché gems and on those rare occasions when a sphene, or a benitoite, or some such curiosity is found in a jewel it was probably made in his workshop.

7. 'Yes he must open the box. It gave with a small jerk, and there lay a dogs collar, made of small flexible plates of pure beaten gold mounted on Russian Leather all of the finest workmanship.' Elinor Glynn, *Three Weeks*, 1907.

Pearls equalled the diamond in value and esteem and the two were often set side by side in the same jewel. Freshwater pearls from a variety of North American mussel occurred in a multitude of random shapes, perfect for representing fishes, flowers, chickens, comic faces and the like (Colour Plate IIIg).

The Victorian lapidary confined himself to a very limited range of cutting styles: the rose, the brilliant, the pear-shaped pendeloque and the cabochon. Other styles existed but there was little demand for them until about 1903. There was the marquise, a boat-shaped brilliant as its other name, navette, implies. The elegantly tapered form of the marquise looks perfect on the finger and many rings were made in which a diamond cut like this was surrounded by a thread-like border of calibré-cut stones. A similar effect was created more cheaply with a thin border of enamel, in white, blue, crimson or oyster grey and gems were often set like this.

As the name suggests a calibré gem is cut to measure to suit the requirements of a particular design and usually takes the form of a tiny square or oblong. The term calibré-cut is only applied to coloured stones: diamonds cut in this way are called 'baguettes'.

The briolette is an adaptation of the rose: a sphere, peardrop or ovoid covered with triangular facets. Diamond briolettes are usually cut from flawed or yellowish stones as this multiplicity of reflecting facets helps to mask their faults, but far from dimming the attractiveness of a briolette these shortcomings seem to enhance it with the appearance of a delicious glittering sultana. Diamond briolettes were used in a variety of ways, hung at intervals on a fine platinum longchain, on a pair of girandole earrings, or close together in a fringe at the ends of a diamond ribbon-bow brooch.

Other gems were cut in this way besides the diamond; aquamarine and even emerald briolettes were mounted in the simplest possible way as pendent earrings, and briolettes of rock crystal, amethyst, citrine and aquamarine quite as big as a chandelier drop were used to finish off a sautoir of pearl, chain or moiré silk ribbon.

In the nineteenth century the domed cabochon cut was used for opaque or translucent stones—garnets and occasionally amethysts were the only significant exceptions. The oriental influences which shaped so many Edwardian fashions meant that rubies, sapphires and emeralds were now occasionally cut as cabochons and in 1902 Benson's were advertising 'Delhi Durbar' jewellery set with emeralds and rubies cut 'Indian fashion'.[8]

Opals were often cut in a way which conformed to no particular style, but sawn into thin slices and trimmed to form flower petals and the wings of diamond-bodied butterflies or dragonflies. Hancock's seemed to make a speciality of this kind of work.

8. *Illustrated London News*, 6 December 1902.

The Edwardian Period—1900 to 1914

ART NOUVEAU AND JUGENDSTIL

Art nouveau came late to fashionable London and it was not until 1900 that its influence was truly felt. Even then the more extravagant excesses of René Lalique never went down very well with the fashionable Englishwoman who shunned them as morbid and decadent. The *fin de siècle* mood which engendered them, however, was felt here as it was everywhere else in Europe. Imagine, for example, an evening gown of 1901—in vermilion tulle folded about the body like a chrysalis, with a string of diamonds for one shoulder-strap, and a chain of poppies sprinkled with

18. *A turquoise and diamond* BROOCH *showing the influence of art nouveau*

diamond dewdrops for the other; the limp petals of a black poppy formed the sleeves with—delightfully lascivious touch—'an interval of white arm visible between it and the shoulder straps'.[9]

The British jeweller was quick to adapt art nouveau to his own purposes, and many pendants and necklaces show the curiously liquid scrolls which above all characterized the new fashion (Plate 18), and many buckles and buttons in particular were stamped in silver with the dreaming girls, the nenuphars and bullrushes of the new iconography.

The retailer also used the art nouveau tag as a marketing device and many novelties were offered to the public as 'new art' which were in truth neither new nor artistic. Certainly anything at all in enamel was hailed as art nouveau, although the

9. *Illustrated London News,* 5 January 1901.

19. (left) *A silver and haematite jugendstil* BROOCH

20. (above) *A diamond* BROOCH *showing jugendstil influence*

great discovery of the Parisian art nouveau jeweller, the miraculously beautiful plique-à-jour enamel, was seldom used in a British commercial workshop.

By 1907 the British public was tired of art nouveau, although its influence was still to be felt for another decade or more.

By one of those odd round trips peculiar to the decorative arts, the angularities and perpendicularities of the Glasgow school of design reached London—via Vienna, Pforzheim and Berlin (Plate 19). Under the guise of jugendstil, the Scottish pedigree of these robust, satisfying designs is not hard to trace. The Anglo-German firm of Murrle Bennet introduced a whole range of jugendstil jewels in the years before the First World War (Colour Plate IIIa), and although they were too far ahead of their time to catch on widely and permanently, the ideas which informed them spread as pervasively as a drop of ink in a jar of water. It was these ideas which, as much as anything else, contributed to that underlying discipline which is the great strength of Edwardian design (Plate 20).

REVIVALS OF EARLIER STYLES

Like the Victorians, the Edwardians looked back into the past for ideas, but they did so more selectively and with a great sense of chic. The Victorians embraced nearly every period, historical and archaeological, with reckless promiscuity—Assyrian,

The Edwardian Period—1900 to 1914

Egyptian, classical, gothic and Renaissance—all was grist to the jeweller's mill. The twentieth-century woman was more particular and chose only those styles which suited her temperament and the spirit of her times, and most designs seem to have been borrowed from the period with which the Edwardians had most in common— the eighteenth and, to a lesser degree, the early nineteenth centuries.

For a year or so after 1900 that old chestnut the Irish ring-brooch continued to be worn, often in a form so remote from its Celtic origin as to be pavé set with diamonds, and also jewelled and enamelled buckles of equally dubious pedigree which some enterprising jeweller had christened 'Kells'.

There can be no doubt, though, that it was the Louis Quinze style which provided the jeweller with most ideas, for the lightness and asymmetry of these designs has much in common with art nouveau. Rococo cartouches with borders of diamond scrolls, enclosing a cluster or some other simple motif on an open latticework pinned with tiny diamonds, made very successful brooches and pendants and the same idea was adapted for bracelets and the centres of collars (Plate 21). The latticework background which was worked into so many different jewels (Colour Plate IIIf) was later varied and refined into the saw-piercing which was to be one of the most appealing features of the late Edwardian jeweller's art. Eighteenth century hearts with accompanying ribbon bows, crowns or true lovers' knots were made in enamels of almost every colour and set with diamonds or pearls (Colour Plate IVc).

The marquise designs for rings and brooches, which first appeared in the late eighteenth century, are some of the prettiest and most wearable ever devised and there is no need to seek a reason for their revival. The marquise design had an oval, octagonal, shield or most typically, a boat-shaped panel of royal-blue enamel edged with rose diamonds and with a cluster or a single stone superimposed at its centre (Plate 22). Sometimes the border was emphasized with a thread of opaque white enamel (Colour Plate IVg) and there were other variations—a sprinkling of tiny rose diamonds over the surface of the enamel for instance. It is not always easy to tell the Edwardian versions from the originals, but later versions may show a proliferation of engraved scrollwork at the back of the bezel and the hoop may be brought on to the bezel with forked shoulders instead of faired into it with smooth taper. Most blue-enamel brooches and pendants in the marquise style are of the later period. The firm of Child and Child made a speciality of this kind of work along with other pretty little fancies of the late eighteenth century. Their work can be recognized by the signature on the reverse—C.C. and a flower. In 1910 Benson's were proclaiming their 'reproductions of the beautiful models worn by the old French noblesse of the eighteenth Century',[10] and simultaneously the Goldsmiths' and Silversmiths' Company were advertising marquise rings and brooches.

10. *Illustrated London News*, 17 December 1910.

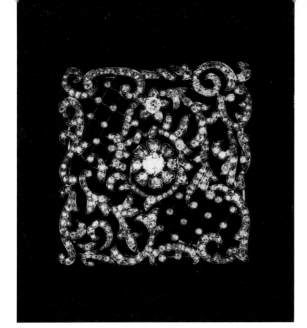

21. *A diamond* BROOCH *in rococo style, probably adapted from a collar slide*

22. *A diamond, blue-enamel and pearl* PENDANT *in eighteenth-century classical style, c.1900*

Far and away the cleverest and most versatile interpreters of historical styles were the Giulianos. Carlo Giuliano was a Neapolitan who came to London sometime in the 1850s and whose pastiches of Renaissance and classical jewels were among the most brilliant of their time. His sons, Carlo and Arthur, succeeded him in the business on his death in 1895 and had the good fortune to retain the services of Pasquale Novissimo as designer. These later jewels of the Giulianos were the finest the family produced and although still inspired by the Renaissance they capture the mood of nineteen-hundred to perfection. Airy confections of black and white enamel scrollwork, lightly frosted with diamonds, their charm is irresistible but never obvious (Colour Plate IVh).

Shoebuckles, often of impressive size and closely modelled on Georgian originals, returned to favour in 1912. One Russian lady at a white cross charity ball in London wore black shoes with diamond buckles and diamond-studded heels, although for 'diamonds' one should probably read 'paste' in this kind of fashion report.[11]

Early nineteenth-century styles were now just old enough to be interesting. There seems to have been an unwritten law of fashion which invested the things which grandmother wore with all the magic of a bygone age, while the fashions that mother wore were merely passé. The recent tidal wave of nostalgia seems to have swept away any such ideas and we now regard the things of little more than a decade ago with the reverend affection it once took half a century to evoke.

11. *Illustrated London News*, 1 February 1912.

The Edwardian Period—1900 to 1914

Very soon after 1900 several jewel fashions were revived from the first half of the previous century whilst anything which smacked of the high Victorian was shunned like the plague. The taste for amethysts was expressed in a revival of those brooches of the 1830s in which a fair-sized amethyst was mounted in a double border of half pearls. It is seldom easy to distinguish these from the originals as they are alike in every particular, even down to the colour of the gold. Sometimes, however, the Edwardian jeweller yields to the temptation to put a more serviceable hook with a patent safety-catch on the brooch fitting and this, provided it is not a replacement, will give the game away.

There was at this time even a half-hearted attempt to revive that very distinctive gold filigree work of the eighteen-twenties known to the collector as 'cannetille', but the twentieth-century jeweller seems to have lost the knack for it and the gold scrollwork is both too spare and too coarse to be convincing (Plate 23).

Between 1820 and 1840 brooches and lockets were often given a border of gold chased with roses, sea shells and feather scrolls. This idea too was revived, also without outstanding success, on cheap brooches and on those round, watch-like pendants with a glass miniature-compartment at the centre. A somewhat similar locket, originating from around 1800, with a miniature of a lock of hair mounted under crystal within a crescent-like border of diamonds was also revived with happier results.

Not only were old fashions resuscitated, but jewel caskets were ransacked for antiques—it became smart to 'do something clever' with an old thing of grandmamma's. The big shell-cameos of the forties were given a new lease of life as belt buckles. The huge pendent earrings of the same period were used to finish off the ends of a longchain and antique pendants of every description from the age of Cellini onwards were worn on a slender chain at the breast.

EASTERN INFLUENCES AND THE RUSSIAN BALLET

By 1903 other influences were making themselves felt, more powerful, more far-reaching and yet more subtle than any others, for at this time we see beginning one of those marvellous transfusions of oriental influence which from the earliest historical times have periodically revitalized Western art. Reasons for it are not hard to find, for events in the newly awakening East were never out of the newspapers for long. Two coronations in 1902 and 1910 meant two Imperial durbars resplendent with caparisoned elephants and jewelled subject princes. Japan's unexpected victory over Russia in 1905, and the barbarities of the Boxer rebellion and its suppression made certain that European eyes were kept glancing somewhat uneasily towards the

23. A gold, emerald and diamond NECKLACE *in imitation of early nineteenth-century cannetille work*

East. It was not of course this brawling infant East of Sun Yat Sen and Mahatma Ghandi that aroused the Western imagination, but the ancient orient of Haroun al Raschid and Kublai Khan: the morninglands of Flecker and Rimsky-Korsakov, of houris and memluks and the golden road to Samarkand.

The Delhi durbars brought a revived interest in Indian jewellery for which there had already been something of a vogue in the eighteen-eighties. J. W. Benson advertised their emerald, ruby and diamond 'Delhi Durbar' jewellery in 1902; portraits of the old Mogul rajahs were avidly studied for fashion ideas, inspiring, in 1910, Paisley turbans trimmed with loops of pearls and feather aigrettes.

In 1908 a little talisman was put on the market as a Christmas novelty. According to Elkington's, who made one in gold and half pearls, its name, swastika, was

Sanskrit for 'good luck'. There was nothing particularly sinister about the swastika at this time—James Elroy Flecker chose it as the blazer badge for his two-man Praxiteles club which, although silly and perverse, was probably no more than mildly wicked. Swastika jewels were certainly very popular as tiepins, brooches and pendants, and were worn for a long time.

Japan had already made herself felt in the decorative arts in the latter part of the previous century when the West re-established contact, and her contribution to art nouveau and the Arts and Crafts movement was considerable. On the orthodox section of the trade, however, her influence was quite small in early twentieth-century Britain. Those gold bangles made to resemble a hoop of bamboo are said to have originated in this way and some jewels were set with decorative plaques of inlaid gold and patinated base metal.

The discoveries of Sir Flinders Petrie started an Egyptian craze which was to gather momentum right on through the nineteen-twenties. Many jewels were based on magical and religious symbols from the ancient kingdoms of the Nile. In 1906 Benson's made a speciality of 'Ankh' jewels in which the Ankh, supposedly symbolizing long life, was arranged with a 'nefer' for good luck. Ankh jewels took many forms: brooches, charms, bracelets, cufflinks, rings and pendants embellished with enamels, diamonds or demantoid garnets (Plate 24). The sistrum, a kind of rattle said to have been used by the priestesses to scare away evil, was also used in jewellery. The Association of Diamond Merchants introduced in 1906 a bracelet

24. (above) An 'Ankh' BROOCH set with diamonds

25. (right) A 'Teta' BRACELET in beads of gold, carved amethyst and turquoise

34

26. A 'Ballet Russe'
PENDANT *in diamonds*
suggesting the eye of a
peacock's feather

which they claimed to be a copy of the jewel found on the mummy of Queen Teta: fashioned from beads of amethyst, turquoise and gold it retailed at £7 15s (Plate 25).

Towards the end of the Edwardian era, the arrival in Paris and London of Diaghilev's Russian ballet fanned the flirtation with the orient into a full-blown passion. Its influence on jewel fashions was oblique and unobtrusive, but no less profound for that: to an enquiring eye the signs are as clear as a spoor to the hunter. At a hospital charity ball on 18 May 1911, the firm of Cartier gave a two-hundred-and-fifty guinea pendant to the girl in the prettiest dress. The design of the jewel was of seminal interest, for its oval outline confined two ruthlessly stylized lotus flowers set base to base, foreshadowing the innumerable beautiful designs on the same theme which were to prove so successful after the First World War.

The orientalism of 1911 was never obvious: an allusion to a cusped arch, the dome of a minaret or the eye of a peacock plume (Plate 26), the mere hint of the double volute of a Chinese ju-i, and yet the designs, traced out with ethereal delicacy in platinum and diamonds and fringed with seductively swaying pendants seem to breathe the fragrances of sandalwood and jasmine (Colour Plate I).

It is paradoxical that Poiret's jupes-culottes should have aroused such intense and chauvinistic male passions when the fashion originated in the submissively female milieu of the harem. Nevertheless, the first women to wear them were chased into the safety of a shop by a male mob; in Madrid extra police had to be called in to cope with the disturbances and the pope ordered priests to refuse absolution to any women wearing one. Poiret intended them to be worn with jewelled anklets and while these do not appear to have been very popular, other jewels of the harem undoubtedly were. The slave bangle, designed to be worn on the upper arm rather than the wrist had a utilitarian as well as a decorative purpose in keeping a long glove in place. The simplest were no more than a hoop of gold; others were set with circular-cut diamonds or calibré-cut coloured stones or onyx.

The bob was worn in the middle of the forehead like the early Victorian ferronnière. A portrait of Eleanor Glynn by de Laszlo shows her wearing a pear-shaped sapphire like a third blue eye in the middle of her forehead hanging from a similar stone pinned in her copper-coloured hair; matching earrings complete the ensemble. A fashion correspondent reports: 'I have seen a fine emerald drop worn as a bob-jewel on the brow depending by a short fine platinum chain from a flat gold bandeau supported on emerald green tulle drawn over the top of the brow.'[12]

LATE EDWARDIAN CLASSICISM

In 1910 the fashionable woman's silhouette changed dramatically and jewellery styles took an equally sudden change in direction. It was a change not only of quality, but also of quantity and women no longer littered themselves with ornaments like the medals on a musical-comedy general. Poiret himself remarked that to dress a woman is not to cover her with ornaments, but to underscore the endowments of her body, to bring out and stress them.

There were economic reasons for change as well as the obvious aesthetic ones. At any one time there is a finite amount of cash to be spent on luxuries and an increasing amount of it was now being used on furs and motor cars, the new status symbols of the twentieth century. But in any case the slimmer fashion line could no longer sustain the elaborate displays of earlier years.

Designs changed, becoming formal and two dimensional with a tangy foretaste of the twenties about them. It might almost be said that the twenties really began in 1910. The reasons for the change were partly technical, for many of the new designs would have been impossible in any other medium but platinum which to the British jeweller was still something of a novelty. As far back as the eighteenth century it was recognized that diamonds look best in a setting of white metal. Silver was then the only possible choice and ladies were willing to put up with the unsightly marks it left on their skin and clothing. Towards 1800 jewellers learned to get the best of both worlds by backing the silver setting with a thin layer of gold, and until the present century diamonds were nearly always set like this.

12. *Illustrated London News*, 19 August 1913.

The French had been experimenting with platinum for some time, but it was not until 1906 that the British jeweller began to make significant use of it. It took him another three years to understand the unique properties of the metal and make the most of them. Platinum is heavy, hard to work and difficult to solder, but its brilliant untarnishable whiteness and great structural strength far outweighed these disadvantages, and it began steadily and surely to oust the gold-and-silver setting for diamonds. The strength of platinum meant that it took less metal to hold a stone safely in place, and settings became so dainty that they were scarcely visible from the front.

In spite of the weight of the metal so little of it was needed to produce a soundly engineered mount that there was a distinct gain in lightness. This in itself extended the jeweller's range, allowing him to make large brooches which were still light enough to be worn on flimsy fabrics.

The hardness of platinum enabled the jeweller, by using a piercing-saw with a blade little thicker than a hair, to fret the metal into lace-like patterns. As much as anything else it is the quality of this saw-piercing which distinguishes the jewellery made between 1909 and 1914 from that of any other period. It is to be seen at its best in the so-called 'plaque pendants' which first appeared in 1910. Usually in the form of a round medallion (although square and octagonal designs are not unknown), the finest of these jewels are as delicate and diverse as frost flowers (Plates 27, 28). Even the cheaper versions in gold, pearls and coloured stones are very appealing (Plate 29).

27. *A saw-pierced platinum and diamond plaque* PENDANT

28. *A saw-pierced platinum and diamond plaque* PENDANT

29. *A gold, half-pearl and peridot flower* PENDANT

*30. An enamel and rose-
diamond* WATCH

Particularly interesting to the collector is the plaque pendant of diamond openwork with interchangeable backgrounds of variously tinted guilloché enamel, allowing the wearer to ring the changes according to the colour of her mood or her dress. The little discs of enamel are usually in delicate shades like lemon, redcurrant, lilac or dove grey and almost invariably include one of gunmetal black for mourning (Colour Plate IVb).

The Edwardian jeweller used his enamel discreetly, a dab of colour on petals or plumage (Colour Plate IVa), or a subdued background to the brilliance of diamonds (Colour Plate IVg). Enamel was often guilloché, fired over a mechanically engraved pattern of intersecting spirals (Plate 30, Colour Plate IIIl). The prettiest watches of the period are more jewel than timepiece, worn as pendants on a long slender chain, the spherical, pear or oval-shaped case in softly glowing guilloché enamel candied with rose diamonds (Colour Plate IVf). Enamel is frequently applied in more than one layer and the Edwardian jeweller sometimes fired one tint upon another, flavouring the work with a faint and delicious opalescence (Colour Plate Va).

Earrings, which had been of little significance for some years, returned towards the end of 1911 and became almost as popular as they had been in mid-Victorian times

38

without reaching quite the same immense proportions. During the first few years of the century earrings had been neat and unobtrusive—a simple cluster worn close to the ear or a chaste pearl drop hung below it. At this time screw fittings were invented which clamped the jewel to the lobe making piercing unnecessary. Designs were quite varied but most were of the pendent variety: loops of pearls, coloured stones hanging from ribbon bows and chains of diamonds, diamond tassels, chandeliers and slim lance-like drops, aquamarine briolettes and pear-shaped uncut emeralds.

The aigrette, which was introduced in the late nineties, was given a new lease of life in 1910. In spite of the protests of bird lovers and the personal example of the queen, who refused to wear the fine white plumage of the egret, the little herons were hunted down in their thousands. A cheaper, and, for the naturalist at least, more acceptable substitute for the precious feathers was a brush of spun-glass filaments and Poiret used this ornament in several of his designs. The plume of the aigrette was set in a diamond holder of wheel, lyre, winged, or crescent design, and in 1910 it was usually worn on a bandeau, Red Indian fashion, although it could be at the front, the side or the back of the head. When in the upright position it was called a lancer plume, but a particularly dashing style required the aigrette to be worn over the left ear slanting downwards like a carpenter's pencil.

To a large degree, the bandeau replaced the tiara and the diadem, those beetling cliffs of diamonds which overshadowed even the gayest occasion (Plate 31).It was a young style that suited the new, slender fashion line. Some were frothy confections entwined from chains of diamond flowers, others were pierced with classical key-fret or anthemion designs and almost austere in their simplicity.

31. *A diamond* BANDEAU *decorated with garlands and saw-piercing*

The Edwardian Period—1900 to 1914

Ribbons of black moiré silk were an important ingredient of many jewels. A ribbon like this secured at throat or wrist with a little slide of white enamel bearing the owner's initials in rose diamonds was a jewel in itself; a slightly more elaborate version might have a diamond edging to the ribbon, and the initials on a heart at the centre (Plate 32). A longer, slimmer ribbon could form a sautoir with a crystal briolette as a pendant. A more elegant sautoir of black ribbon was sprigged with rose-diamond forget-me-nots.

In these as in other jewels, the jeweller and the dressmaker seem to meet on common ground: in 1910 black velvet bows were given a diamond trimming and a

32. A BRACELET *of diamonds and black moiré ribbon*

couple of years later J. C. Vickery transfixed the bow with a curious kind of brooch, a stout platinum pin with a decorative motif at each end, one of them removable to allow the point to be stuck through the fabric. This jewel, the sûreté pin, was to become fashionable after the First World War.

Fresh ideas came crowding into fashion in 1910: new techniques, new sources of inspiration, new shapes. There was the rainbow, a simple arch, usually with another motif hanging below it, which may have been copied by the commercial jeweller from his separated brethren in the Arts and Crafts movement (Plate 33). The rainbow idea certainly has a ring of Arts and Crafts optimism about it. There is a suggestion, too, of Arts and Crafts medievalism about the trefoils and quatrefoils that

33. *A platinum and diamond* STOMACHER BROOCH *of rainbow design with saw-pierced decoration*

34. *A platinum and diamond* BROOCH *in a quatrefoil design*

abounded just now although these simple organic motifs are among the hardy annuals of the designer's repertoire in any case (Plate 34).

An upturned kite best describes one of the popular motifs of these and the immediate post-war years, a sort of bottom heavy lozenge with the sharpest angle at the top which was very popular for pendants and earrings. A pendant like this was marketed under the name of the 'handkerchief', presumably because it remotely resembled a folded pocket-handkerchief with a dainty lace trimming (Plate 35).

The neo-classical style of 1910 did not just arrive overnight; it had been developed and refined by a generation of jewellers over twenty years. As in true classical jewellery, emphasis was on the head and neck and it is the necklaces and pendants

35. *A platinum and diamond handkerchief* PENDANT, *finely pierced*

36. A diamond STOMACHER BROOCH *by* CARTIER

which show the style off best. There had been garlands, key-frets, swags, palmettes and ivy leaves in the jewels of other ages, now they were expressed with an ethereal, almost uncanny lightness of touch which only platinum, the magic metal could make possible. Luscious garlands dewed with diamonds hung from chains of collet-set brilliants as supple as a piece of string while diamond tassels swayed below (Plate 36). Movement was essential and tassels were as popular in jewels as they were in costume into which Poiret had introduced them as a focus of coquetry.

Undoubtedly the whole neo-classical style was French in origin and inspiration, just as the best of everything Edwardian was French. And yet grave and gay, it is rarely spoiled by the mechanical chilliness which sometimes infects French designs. No one will deny that King Edward's entente cordiale revived and transformed the decorative arts and breathed a new life into them that even the austere George V and his German queen could not suppress. There were three monarchs on the throne between 1900 and 1914, yet for us this always was and always will be the Edwardian age.

42

2 · The Great War

The outbreak of war had a disastrous effect on the British jewellery trade. Platinum was a strategic raw material, vital as a catalyst for the manufacture of nitric acid for explosives and for engine magnetos, and the government lost no time in commandeering all the available stocks and forbade any dealing in it.

For the first fourteen months of hostilities the gem trade was completely paralysed. The price of diamonds in Amsterdam and Antwerp fell by twenty per cent and more and in the face of this De Beers had no alternative but to shut down production until prices stabilized.

At the cheaper end of the trade the market was flooded with so-called military jewellery. It was, almost without exception, trivial and in the worst conceivable taste, and yet it cannot fail to interest the collector because it was so much the product of its time. More than any other recent historical event, the First World War has become part of our national folklore and the Angels of Mons, the disappearance of Kitchener, and the Russians-with-snow-on-their-boots are all the stuff of which legends are made. Inconsequential although these little trinkets are they tell us a good deal about the tragic losses, the scoundrelly patriotism, the hysteria, the propaganda and the privations of 1914–18.

War in the air lent additional point to the aeronautical jewellery of the pre-war years, but now the subjects were fighter planes and observation blimps and as often as not the legend 'R.F.C.' or the eagle of the service was added to them. On similar lines were those brooches representing a tank (Plate 37), a battleship, or a submarine (Plate 38).

The indiscriminating fortunes of modern war led to the curious fatalistic belief in the shell with your regimental number on it and also to the opposite and equally primitive philosophy of luck. Innumerable charms, talismans and amulets were invented by enterprising, if cynical, manufacturers. A Mons Angel amulet charm was made in both silver and gold by H. C. Freeman of Hatton Garden either as a pendant or a brooch (Plate 37). Arthur J. Pepper of Birmingham advertised brooches designed around a wishbone and a horseshoe and inscribed 'Cheerio'.

Inevitably lockets for a photograph were very popular. White and Redgrove made

Mr. Lloyd George's
LUCKY MASCOT

There is one million to be sold among the munition workers.

SPEED UP
MUNITIONS
EMBLEM.

Registered No. 651360.

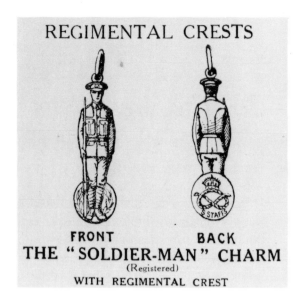

REGIMENTAL CRESTS

FRONT   BACK
THE "SOLDIER-MAN" CHARM
(Registered)
WITH REGIMENTAL CREST

Peace
HATH ITS CHARM

AT THE *11th* HOUR OF THE *11th* DAY OF THE *11th* MONTH THE *"Dove"* SYMBOLIC OF *Peace* TOOK FLIGHT ON ITS MISSION.

REG. No. 665772

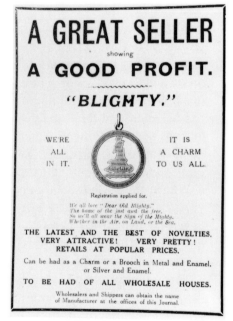

A GREAT SELLER
showing
A GOOD PROFIT.

"BLIGHTY."

WE'RE   IT IS
ALL   A CHARM
IN IT.   TO US ALL.

Registration applied for.

We all love "Dear Old Blighty,"
The home of the just and the free,
So we'll all wear the Sign of the Mighty,
Whether in the Air, on Land, or the Sea.

THE LATEST AND THE BEST OF NOVELTIES.
VERY ATTRACTIVE!   VERY PRETTY!
RETAILS AT POPULAR PRICES.

Can be had as a Charm or a Brooch in Metal and Enamel, or Silver and Enamel.

TO BE HAD OF ALL WHOLESALE HOUSES.

Wholesalers and Shippers can obtain the name of Manufacturer at the offices of this Journal.

THE KAISER UNDER THE HAT.

Putting the Hat on the Kaiser.
The New Registered
DOUGHBOY Charm,
Regd. No. 664613.
To celebrate the Victory of the Americans.
Made in Silver and 9ct. Gold.
Write for Samples.

37. Extracts from advertisements published in the Watchmaker, Jeweller and Silversmith *during the First World War*

signet rings with locket bezels: 'Sell them to the soldier' exhorts their advertisement in the trade press, 'Sell them to his wife: let them both wear babies portrait.'[1] That this firm had no time for the soft sell is apparent from another telling line from their ace copywriter, this time advertising a mourning brooch: 'It is obvious that this jewellery will sell wherever partings are endured for the allied cause.'[2] Another manufacturer, J. W. Tiptaft, made lockets inscribed 'His country called—he answered!' Even the munition worker did not escape the jeweller's patriotic zeal, for 'Mr Lloyd George's Lucky Mascot' a winged artillery shell with the stirring motto 'Speed up Munitions' was especially designed with them in mind (Plate 37).

War did nothing to decrease the flow of novelty jewels which now flooded on the market, dafter and more numerous than ever. The potato shortage resulted in the potato charm; the 'Blighty' charm was an outline map of Britain (Plate 37) and the 'doughboy charm' of 1918 represented the Kaiser wearing instead of his eagle helmet, an American soldier's wide-brimmed hat (Plate 37). The 'fumsup' charm represented an obese infant giving the Tommy's thumbs-up salutation. This absurd trinket could be bought in anything from plain silver to palladium and diamonds. Major Scott, captain of the airship R84 was in the habit of carrying a fumsup charm. Even the armistice was celebrated with an appropriate novelty jewel: a dove of peace flying across the number eleven (Plate 37).

Regimental-badge brooches were produced in their thousands, some expensively made in diamonds and fine enamels, others of inlaid silver and tortoiseshell for only a few shillings (Plate 38). Regimental buttons were mounted up into brooches with a photograph of the 'soldier sweetheart' at the back in a glass miniature-compartment (Plate 38). The soldier-man charm represented an infantryman at attention with his regimental insignia in a plaque at the reverse (Plate 37).

The wearing of jewels in the form of military decorations was forbidden, but this taboo did not extend to the ribbon which was frequently mounted under glass as a brooch—much as a lock of hair used to be worn. Henry Griffiths and Sons of Birmingham sold 18-carat gold rings enamelled with regimental colours.

Air raids by German Zeppelins plunged London into the first wartime blackout and in 1916 four patents were filed for luminous jewellery. When the first airship was shot down at Cuffley, wire salvaged from the wreckage was made into a bracelet which the queen gave to the Red Cross who raised two hundred pounds for it.

There was a boom in wrist watches, the dials suitably protected by a grille against the accidents of trench warfare, and identification bracelets with a choice of finishes, either silver plated, oxidized or khaki had a ready sale.

1. *Watchmaker, Jeweller and Silversmith*, March 1918.
2. *Watchmaker, Jeweller and Silversmith*, September 1916.

38. *Military jewellery inspired by the First World War*

Even in 1916 when the war was being fought at its fiercest there is some evidence that the bugbear of German competition which had haunted the British jewellery trade for the last forty years had still not been laid to rest. In the editorial of the *Watchmaker and Jeweller* of 16 January we read: 'Parliament is at last taking steps to put a finish to Germans doing business here . . . total exclusion for Germans and German goods is the allied motto, and a very proper one too.' An uncomfortable reversal of the situation which had obliged Napoleon to import English cloth for his own soldiers' uniforms.

Later, although the ban on dealing in unfashioned platinum remained in force, trade in finished goods was permitted. In any case by this time the trade had found an acceptable substitute in palladium, a slightly paler, brighter metal which had the advantage of being lighter than platinum. As the war of attrition dragged on things began to look brighter for the jeweller. War was generating a breed of men who, since armies were ever invented, was as much its creature as the soldier and the armourer—the profiteer. Men who had grown wealthy almost overnight on war contracts and the black market revelled in the vulgarity for which Siegfried Sassoon so roundly lambasted them. The champagne and the diamonds poured out in a frothing, glittering tide and De Beers revenue doubled in a single year. The Russian émigré aristocrats who came to this country in 1917 found a ready market for the jewels they brought with them, just as the French had done in 1789.

3 · Arts and Crafts

According to Eric Gill, Arts and Crafts, socialism and the new theologies were 'revolts against the devilish state of England'. Whatever one's personal view of the spiritual condition of England at the turn of the century, Gill was not exaggerating about the revolutionary character of Arts and Crafts. William Morris and his kin were out, not only to make beautiful and useful things, but to recreate society in the process. Modern man was to be redeemed and exalted by toil and purified by the disciplines of his craft.

They believed that history had taken a wrong turn sometime in the Middle Ages, that the Renaissance had been an aberration and the Industrial Revolution a disaster. There was a passionate yearning for the intensity and single mindedness of the Middle Ages, and medievalism runs strong and deep through Arts and Crafts philosophy in consequence. If mankind was to be saved he should retrace his steps and make a fresh start, and this incessant worrying back to the grass roots of everything is the key to all the Arts-and-Craftsmen made and did, the way they learned their trade, organized their workshops and lived their lives. It filled their work with innocence and life and bedevilled it with the most embarrassing imperfections.

Arts and Crafts philosophy rejected the machine, capitalism, the industrial society and above all the city. W. R. Lethaby wrote of London: 'A half hundred miles, once wood and cornfield, roofed over, where we grow sickly like grass under a stone, intersected by innumerable avenues, all asphalt, lamp posts and wires. Little good it serves to wail or rail yet at times most of us must shiver with despair and examine means of escape like creatures untamed to a cage, longing for the time when the weeds and flowers biding their time under the paving stones will again expand to the rain and wave to the breezes.'[1] This curiously poignant image of imprisoned and triumphant nature is a recurring theme in Arts and Crafts work and thinking.

The Englishman's love of his countryside, on the other hand, assumes an almost mystical significance. Life on the land and in the village seemed to offer to the artist-

---

1. W. R. Lethaby, 'Of Beautiful Cities', in *Art and Life*, London 1897.

I. A diamond and pearl PENDANT *in Ballet Russe style, c.1910.*
See page 35

II. A ruby and diamond BROOCH *set with brilliant and rose-cut diamonds and calibré-cut*
rubies. See page 21

III. (a) *A gold, tourmaline and blister-pearl* BRACELET *by* MURRLE BENNET. See page 29
 (b) *A ruby and diamond* NECKLACE. See pages 22, 25
 (c) *A gold, peridot and pearl bee* BROOCH. See page 21
 (d) *A diamond, enamel and pearl snake and new-moon* BROOCH.
 (e) *A rose-diamond and guilloché enamel ivy-leaf* BROOCH. See page 38
 (f) *A gold, half-pearl and amethyst* PENDANT. See page 30
 (g) *A gold and Mississippi-pearl flower* BROOCH. See page 27
 (h) *A gold, enamel and pearl clover-leaf and horseshoe* BROOCH. See page 23
 (i) *A gold, half-pearl and demantoid-garnet new-moon and monkey* BROOCH. See page 25

IV. *(a) An enamel and diamond flower* PENDANT. *See page 38*

(b) A platinum and diamond plaque PENDANT *with interchangeable enamel plaques.*
See page 38

(c) An enamel and diamond heart BROOCH. *See page 30*

(d) A yellow sapphire and diamond BROOCH. *See page 26*

(e) An opal, diamond and pearl PENDANT *influenced by jugendstil and art nouveau.*
See page 26

(f) An enamel and diamond pendent WATCH. *See page 38*

(g) A pearl, enamel and rose-diamond BROOCH *of heart and lovers'-knot design.*
See pages 30, 38

(h) A gold, enamel, zircon, diamond and pearl BROOCH *by* GIULIANO. *See page 31*

V. *(a) A silver-gilt, moonstone, sapphire and opalescent enamel* NECKLACE *by* CHILD AND
   CHILD. *See page 38*
   (b) A gold, opal, moonstone and enamel PENDANT *by* HENRY WILSON. *See page 60*

VI. *(opposite) Part of a* GIRDLE *of steel and gold set with enamels representing Tristan and
   Isolde, 1896, by* ALEXANDER FISHER. *See page 50*
   Courtesy of the Victoria and Albert Museum

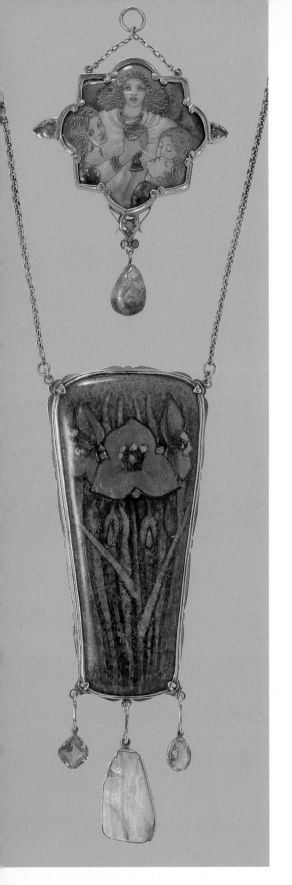

IX. *A silver and plique-à-jour enamel* PENDANT *by* MAY HART. See page 51

VIII. *A gold* PENDANT *set with blister pearls and cabochon gems, the reverse with a relief of the Virgin and Child and inscribed 'Mater Christi', by* HENRY WILSON, *c.1900.* See page 59

VII. (left) (a) *A gold, enamel and pearl* PENDANT *inscribed on the reverse 'The Love Cup 1907', by* PHOEBE TRAQUAIR. See page 72

(b) *A gold* PENDANT *set with an enamel of irises and hung with opal and amethysts by* NELSON AND EDITH DAWSON. See page 50

All courtesy of the Victoria and Albert Museum

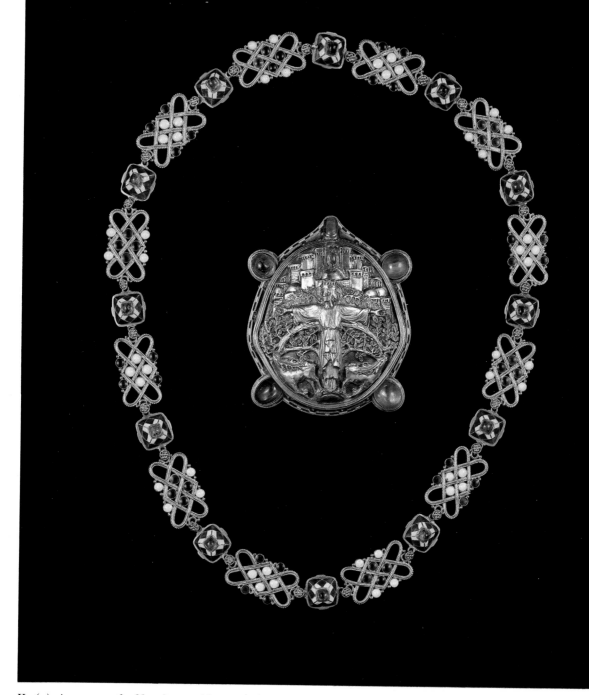

X. (a) A COLLAR *of gold and enamel knot motifs set with emeralds, by* HENRY WILSON,
   c.1905. See page 60
   (b) *A gold, enamel, ruby and emerald* BROOCH PENDANT *with a relief of Christ standing before
   the Holy City, c. 1906. See page 60*
   Courtesy of the Victoria and Albert Museum

XI. *(a)* *A gold and inlaid opal* BROOCH, LIBERTY'S. *See page* 68
    (b) *'Out of the Deep', a gold and enamel* PENDANT *by* PHOEBE TRAQUAIR. *See page* 72
    (c) *A* BRACELET *in gold, fire opal, enamel and Mississippi pearl by* ALFRED JONES.
     See page 73

craftsman the simplicity and innocence he was striving to rediscover. Peasant designs were freely adapted by the jeweller, and the flowers of the woods, meadows and marshes were a constant inspiration to him. The search for simplicity informed even his choice of materials. Gold in an Arts and Crafts jewel is not common and platinum is unheard of. Most work is in silver and the semi-precious stones, moonstones, opals, turquoises, peridots and mother-of-pearl.

ENAMELLING

In the early years of Arts and Crafts little attention was paid to jewellery. Morris did not concern himself with it, although his daughter May made some pleasant pieces. Interest grew fast, however, paralleled by a revival in the art of enamelling which had fallen into neglect since the eighteen-forties. In the mid-eighties a group of students at the Royal College of Art were invited to a demonstration of enamelling by a Monsieur Dalpeyrat of Paris. Among them was *Alexander Fisher* (1864–1936).

Fisher had already experimented with enamel glazes as his father was an enameller on pottery, but this was his introduction to enamelling on metal. Encouraged by Thomas Armstrong, the director of the school, he continued to experiment on his own account and his first attempt was at repairing a damaged enamel at the kitchen fire.

In the jewellery trade at the end of the nineteenth century there was little demand for enamel and consequently for enamellers either. Fisher could find no one in England to teach him the craft—although if he had crossed the channel he would have experienced no such difficulty. Characteristically he taught himself by trial and error, even learning how to make his own enamel as a painter used once to grind his own pigments. 'A student', he wrote, 'ought to feel his material as keenly as he does his subject. He must get inside it so to speak and live at ease there within the bounds set by its limitations.'[2] Practical experiments were combined with a minute study of the finest old work. He admired Byzantine cloisonné because it was so much a part of the surface it decorated like, as he put it, 'a sort of natural metallic growth'. Fisher's enamels have this feeling of wholeness and integrity and seem to fit a jewel as snugly as the iridescent skin of a lizard.

Fisher laid down clear rules for the student's guidance. Of champlevé enamel he says that the outlines should be kept simple, the lines few but thick enough to be seen. Champlevé enamels should neither be much darker than the metal nor much lighter and should be blended and shaded within their boundaries. Areas of metal should be

2. Alexander Fisher, 'The Art of True Enamelling upon Metal', *Studio*, 1901.

decorated with an engraved pattern, the whole idea being to mute and tone down the harsh contrasts inherent in the champlevé technique. Ignorance of these principles was, he believed, the cause of much hardness and tightness in the work of his contemporaries.

The question of scale concerned him: he observed, for example, that translucent enamel used in large areas becomes dull and dark and loses its sparkle, and for this reason he confined its use mainly to jewellery. Preciousness was what he strove for, an essential quality which had for him nothing to do with intrinsic worth—he boasted that his enamels fired clearer and better on copper than most others did on fine gold. The girdle which Fisher made for Lady Horniman has a setting of pierced steel yet it conveys this notion of preciousness more surely than if it were of platinum (Colour Plate VI). Fisher's preciousness is the relationship between line, tone, mass and colour and what he calls the 'special genius of the material'.

He had the true Arts and Crafts passion for the work and believed as a teacher that his first duty was to ignite the same enthusiasm in his students. To him the craft was a kind of priesthood whose adepts needed 'ardent respect for the kind and high office which they have to perform in its daily service'.[3] Fisher was a traditionalist rather than an innovator and the task which he set himself was that of rediscovering the ancient secrets of his craft rather than inventing new methods and techniques.

Nelson Dawson (1859–1941), although he worked at the same time as Fisher, took a different approach. Originally a water-colourist, he first began to work in metals in the early nineties. In 1893 he married Edith Robinson, the start of one of those intensely close working relationships which seemed to blossom so readily at the time. The surfaces of their enamels were deliberately left dull and the texture of the enamel granular and near opaque. The effect, though subdued, was seldom coarse because of the skill with which the design, usually of growing flowers, was organized (Colour Plate VIIb).

Harold Stabler (1872–1945) was a Westmoreland man and he lectured at the Keswick School of Industrial Art before coming down to London where he taught at Sir John Cass College. He and his sculptor wife Phoebe made a delightful series of cloisonné enamels with the help of Mr Kato, a Japanese craftsman. Most of them are in opaque colours, simply mounted as pendants and quite large—often too large to have been worn as jewels. A blue-winged cherub sits with a cockatoo on its chubby fist, the other hand with a finger raised in rebuke, the background of tomato red. Naked children ride chariots drawn by fawns or panthers or sit triumphantly astride dromedaries or polar bears or a tasselled and garlanded bull. The Stablers' enamels were sure and clever and as a designer Harold was to survive into

3. Alexander Fisher, op.cit.

the twenties and thirties and make a significant contribution to British art deco (Plate 39).

Madeleine Martineau who appears to have been a student at Sir John Cass made 18-carat gold sculptural jewellery of some refinement. Her jewels were made to a small scale, in itself unusual in an Arts and Crafts context, and she gave to them a piquant choice of enamel colours; a pendant modelled with the figure of St Cecilia playing a portative has a cloisonné decoration of turquoise, lettuce and amber-tinted enamels.

Few examples exist today of British enamelled jewels in the supremely difficult plique-à-jour technique. A variation of cloisonné, it is called plique-à-jour because

39. A gold and cloisonné enamel BROOCH *by* HAROLD STABLER

the light passes through it like a stained-glass window. A pendant by *May Hart* in the Victoria and Albert Museum is in plique-à-jour style, the surfaces of the enamel domed in an interesting cabochon effect (Colour Plate IX).

A great deal of enamel was made in the years before 1914. Quality varied enormously and much of it was what might be called 'pseudo Arts and Crafts', made by machine in designs of fleshy leaves fired with translucent blues and greens.

THE ART SCHOOLS AND THE BIRMINGHAM STYLE

In a sense the art schools were to the Arts and Crafts movement both creature and creator, and craftsmen who received their training in the schools often came back to teach in them. Many of our art colleges were founded during these years and they are very much a part of the Arts and Crafts movement.

Serious popular art instruction in this country really began with the School of Design, now the Royal College of Art, in 1839. The school grew out of a need to counter foreign industrial competition with better-designed British goods. The intention was to train men, preferably with a practical background in the mill or workshop, to become industrial designers—and the rules of the school specifically excluded any student who wanted to become a painter or a sculptor. In spite of this by the late nineteenth century only a quarter of the students were studying design and the school had won a European reputation for teaching the fine arts, a comment in itself on our attitudes to art in industry. The threat of German industrial competition now made the Board of Education take a good look at the college and its objectives. The design section was strengthened and W. R. Lethaby, one of the great prophets and protagonists of Arts and Crafts, was appointed to lead it.

The Victoria and Albert Museum was a close neighbour to the college — in fact the collection of casts which had been purchased for the students to draw and study eventually formed the nucleus of the museum collection. The opportunities which the museum gave of studying the finest craftsmanship of the past must have been a considerable influence on men like Ramsden, Carr and Fisher. The contribution of the Royal College of Art to the design of jewellery in the twentieth century has been distinctive and lasting and it has left a notable imprint on the Arts and Crafts movement.

Like the Royal College, the Birmingham Vittoria Street School did much for the twentieth-century craft revival and it too grew out of the practical needs of industry. In 1887 the jewellers of Birmingham formed an association, one of whose main objectives was the artistic training of the apprentices working in the city. The Municipal School of Art agreed to fit out workshops for young jewellers so that they could be taught about design and the specialized techniques of the craft under one roof. Technical training was controlled by the Birmingham Jewellers' Association and the artistic side of the course by the school itself. It soon became apparent that the objectives of the two governing bodies were pulling the school in opposite directions and the bewildered students found that what they were doing had little to do with the realities of earning a living at the bench: the artistic training was too academic and the technical training too theoretical and aimed at passing the City and Guilds examination.

In 1901 a fresh start was made in Vittoria Street and R. Catterson Smith, a distinguished artist who had worked with Morris on the Kelmscott Chaucer was made its principal. The new school got off to a good start: Catterson Smith had two firm beliefs: one that the English lad was an artistic animal, second that the craftsman should work directly from nature. Unlike many other teachers of his day he had little time for the slavish and sterile copying of plaster casts. The student was given a sprig of some plant and told to observe and to draw. This emphasis on plant forms is very obvious in the work of those who studied at Vittoria Street in these early years and after 1907 this Birmingham style permeated the whole Arts and Crafts movement.

Birmingham at this time was the heart of the British manufacturing jewellery trade. Much of the jewellery made there was technically very sound and produced with typical Brummagem competence. And yet it was precisely this skill that the Arts and Crafts people criticized with a prudishness which, for us, surrounded by the injection-moulded nastiness of the late twentieth century, is difficult to understand. The argument went thus: modern jewellery is often badly designed and well made, therefore if we forget all we know about technique and start again from scratch, designs will automatically improve. Even if we accepted the premises of this argument, anyone with even the most tenuous grasp of logic will see its fundamental weaknesses and it was this which all too often betrayed the Arts and Crafts movement. Nevertheless, in an oblique way it hit upon an important truth. Professional jewellers were obsessed with technique which at this time reached a level which has never been surpassed, so that at times one finds oneself wondering whether one is looking at a piece of diamond jewellery or a virtuoso study in saw-piercing or diamond setting.

With nihilistic zeal the Arts and Crafts jewellers brainwashed themselves of all that had been learned since Benvenuto Cellini. Using the same argument that stuck artificial moles on the faces of eighteenth-century beauties they protested that blemishes add charm and character. To some degree, of course, this may be true: small irregularities do make the eye travel more slowly over a surface. If the blemish is a dry solder-joint, however, the jewel will simply fall apart. All too often this amateurism made a virtue of incompetence and as much as anything else led to the eventual downfall of British Arts and Crafts.

Arthur and Georgina Gaskin were involved with the Birmingham art schools from the outset. Georgina Evelyn Cave (1868–1934) was an illustrator as well as a skilled silversmith and enamellist. Arthur (1862–1928) was a draughtsman of considerable ability. The couple started making jewellery together around the turn of the century. Their search for the grass roots of their craft seems to have led them at first towards peasant jewellery. A heart-shaped pendant with three drops punched with a simple design and set with turquoise and chrysoprase was probably suggested by the Norwegian *hjertesölje*,[4] and a ring brooch by Georgina in the Cork Arts and Crafts exhibition of 1902 looks as though it could have been inspired by an Algerian design.[5]

Italian traditional jewellery was the strongest influence on their earlier work, and Arthur Gaskin is known to have visited Italy with Joseph Southall in 1897. These designs of branching openwork, which suggest the fragile skeleton of a fallen leaf, foreshadowed and provided a starting point for their mature style which began to emerge around 1905. The transition was as natural and organic as the designs themselves. The early curvilinear designs now sprouted masses of willowy leaves gently punctuated with small flowers, later on inhabited with songbirds. It was an unmistakably English style, modest and beguiling as a cottage garden, but with that

4. 'Modern Design in Jewellery and Fans', edited by Charles Holme, *Studio*, 1902.
5. See *Studio*, Vols. 26–7, 1902.

tang of the south about it, of Provençal herbs and Spanish oranges that flavours the best of Northern European art (Plate 40).

By 1910 the Gaskins were probably the most influential jewellers of the British Arts and Crafts movement and many jewellers, among them Kate M. Eadie, Mrs Hadaway and Margaret Audrey owed a great deal to them. This influence was due not only to their work, but to Arthur Gaskin's appointment as head of the Vittoria Street school of jewellery and silversmithing in 1902.

The Gaskins used enamel in a way that Fisher must have approved of—as sparingly as if it were musk or ambergris; coolly translucent blues and greens that give sap and succulence to leaf and petal. Gems were set in closed collets and usually

40. *A gold and silver* BROOCH *set with opals, half pearls, pink tourmalines and green pastes, signed 'G', by the* GASKINS

semi-precious: topazes, aquamarines, amethysts, baroque pearl, mother-of-pearl, and a great many small drop-shaped stones which appear at a superficial glance to be green tourmalines but turn out to be pastes on a closer examination. A jeweller's preference for a particular gem is often the result of his having come by a parcel of those particular stones.

The Birmingham style undoubtedly owes much to *Bernard Cuzner* (1877–1956) one of the most original spirits of the Arts and Crafts movement. It was intended that Bernard should follow his father into the watch-making trade and he was at first apprenticed to him. Eventually he broke away from the family business and went to work for a Birmingham silversmith, studying at Vittoria Street in the evenings. In 1910 he took over the metalwork department at Birmingham School of Art, Margaret Street.

Cuzner's jewellery was simple, serviceable and, in its day, reasonably priced. He had that understanding of precious metal which allowed it to suggest the design: he placed little reliance on elaborate drawings and often his little jewels seem to have sprung up in the flame of the blowpipe as a thought comes unbidden into the head. Vines tenderly coil and intertwine in designs which at a superficial glance appear to have been suggested by art nouveau, but a closer look will find none of the lurching returns of the Parisian whip-scroll and a definite kinship with honest gothic. Saucy little popinjay birds sit in wreaths of twisted wire and cabochons or perch on top of a horn comb in a splendid coat of enamel plumage. It was said of Cuzner that he never repeated a design and looking at his work one has the feeling that he would not have been able to even if he had tried.

He seldom used saw-piercing, preferring to solder all the different elements together, with wire twists for textural contrast. The energy in these well-knit designs seems to flow from some key nodal-point, usually a cabochon gem, and his work has that medieval flavour which characterized so much of the Margaret Street output at that time.

Fine though the jewels of *W. T. Blackband* were, he is perhaps better known as a teacher and propagandist, not only of the twentieth-century craft revival but of the applied arts as a whole. A Birmingham man born and bred, he was associated with the Vittoria Street school for most of his life. While apprenticed to a local goldsmith he went to evening classes there in the late nineties and took over as principal when Gaskin retired in 1924.

Blackband was devoted to everything that Arts and Crafts stood for and was a passionate anti-consumerist, saddened by the way in which so much fine British talent was squandered on hastening good materials from the factory to the rubbish tip. He was equally vehement in his denunciation of art nouveau which he seems to have held partly responsible for the decline of the Birmingham jewellery trade. Blackband's mature style was formal and masculine and in his decorations of tightly scrolled wire one feels that he is looking back beyond the Middle Ages to a very distant past indeed.

NATURALISM

Throughout the Birmingham style and indeed the whole of Arts and Crafts we glimpse the philosophy of Christopher Dresser, whose fascinating and almost obsessive work *The Art of Decorative Design* (1862) had such a deep influence on his own and on succeeding generations. Dresser has that English passion for flowers which can be so clearly seen in our decorative arts over the centuries. 'If a week is not too long to spend in contemplation of a simple leaf how long should we meditate upon a flower? Say a month. Happy should we be in devoting every hour of the time to the contemplation of a solitary flower, if we thought that we had sagacity sufficient to enable us in that time to perceive and fully understand its beauty.'

This preoccupation with plant forms and structures shows not only in the designs but in the way in which jewels are made. The elements sprout out of and grow into one another like roots, twigs and branches, intertwine and support one another like vines and tendrils. The parts of a jewel are soldered together rather than pierced out

41. A silver, enamel and mother-of-pearl PENDANT *by the* GASKINS, *front and back*

of sheet with the saw. When the Arts and Crafts people talked of 'natural design' this was what they meant (Plate 41).

Although abstract and geometrical designs are rare, apart from the usual architectural conventions, most Arts and Crafts jewels are symmetrical and stylized. *Edgar Simpson*'s designs of leaping fishes and sinewy vines are held in check by strong verticals and solid outlines (Plate 42). He oxidized his silver to tone down its harshness and his enamel was often of a pearly tint scarcely contrasted with the metal itself. Arts and Crafts workers loved these slim dace-like fishes as well as swallows, owls and peacocks. Of the plants they seemed to favour mistletoe, grapevines, the diaphanous seed-pods of honesty and roses, hedgerow briars or the

56

42. *A gold and rose-diamond* PENDANT *by* EDGAR SIMPSON

43. *A black opal, silver and pearl* PENDANT *by* JOSEPH HODEL

lusty cabbage roses that we see in *Joseph Hodel*'s pendant (Plate 43). This jewel is slightly unusual in that it appears to have been cast and sharpened-up with a chisel afterwards rather than hammered-up in repoussé. The human figure makes an occasional appearance in Hodel's jewels as it does throughout Arts and Crafts. Seldom though is the human form stressed or distorted as it so often is in French art nouveau.

Sailing boats are often represented in jewels, as in all the decorative arts, and particularly in the work of the Guild of Handicrafts. They seemed to symbolize the idea of man at one with nature and the elements so important in Arts and Crafts thinking (Plate 44).

44. *An enamel, gold and Mississippi pearl sailing-ship* PENDANT *in the style of the Guild of Handicrafts*

57

ARTS AND CRAFTS MEDIEVAL

The medievalism of Arts and Crafts had nothing to do with nineteenth-century gasworks gothic. Victorian gothic was an architectural style in which the ogives, crockets and quatrefoils of an English cathedral were cannibalized into everything from umbrella stands to coke stoves. The medievalism of Wilson, Cuzner and the Gaskins, although hardly less artificial, grew from a deliberately cultivated state of mind. They thought themselves into the working methods of the Middle Ages and the jewels they made were a more or less natural consequence of the tools, techniques and materials they used.

Omar Ramsden (1873–1939) and *Alwyn Carr* (1872–1940) were both convinced Catholics, which is why so much of their work is of a religious or ceremonial character. Although best known as silversmiths, they made some fine jewels and their work is characterized by a kind of medieval intensity and singleness of purpose. Many of the pendants which they made represented a saint (Plate 45), the designs sometimes quite clearly suggested by the decorative enamelled medallions which centred the silver-mounted maplewood bowls for which they were justly renowned. Unfortunately the partnership broke up when Carr returned from his army service in the First World War. But Ramsden was a shrewd businessman and although bereft of

45. *A silver, garnet, emerald and pearl* PENDANT *representing St Beatrix, dated 1928, by* OMAR RAMSDEN

46. Repoussé silver BELT CLASP *set with moonstones and amethysts by* HENRY WILSON

Carr's very considerable talent he carried on the business until his death in 1939.

The Arts and Crafts movement produced some good jewellers but perhaps only a single great one. *Henry Wilson* (1864–1934) towers so far above his contemporaries that it is not easy to fit him into the scheme of this commentary. Like so many Arts and Crafts designers and jewellers, Wilson was trained as an architect, working for J. D. Sedding and taking over his practice when he died. He seems to have become interested in metalworking around 1890. Gradually he came to spend more and more time in his metalwork shop and his activities there slowly weaned him away from his practice. He taught at the Central and at South Kensington, became president of the Arts and Crafts Exhibition Society and master of the Art Workers' Guild.

Wilson's style is so much his own and owes so little to any of his contemporaries that the only people one can begin to compare him with turn out to have been either his pupils or his imitators. The electric storms of art nouveau sizzle over his head, the angularities of jugendstil leave not a dent, the Glasgow spooks raise not a frisson. He drew his inspiration from the same spring that refreshed Morris, Ruskin, Dresser and the best men of his time—from observed nature and the medieval past. And yet Wilson remains unmistakably himself.

Foliate designs proliferate in his work and no craftsman could express the nature of a plant as he could, its sappy resilience and hidden power; these jewels seem to confine latent energy like the horny casing of a seed. In no sense does he imitate nature, yet his jewels express it as powerfully as a cave painting (Plate 46).

59

Arts and Crafts

Wilson deviated little from his chosen path and never joined in the restless hunt after the novel and outlandish as some of his contemporaries did. He was continually learning and applying new skills, and his work uses a wide repertoire of different techniques, enamelling, lapidary work, casting and repoussé. The symbolism in his work is not just a matter of content, but also of style which is of heraldic formality (Colour Plate Xa). This heraldic feeling is heightened by the courses of chequered or herringbone cloisonné enamel which confine the design (Colour Plate Xb).

The back of a jewel is often the real test of a craftsman's skill and to the trained eye is more revealing than the front. The good jeweller finishes the reverse with care and affection, the bad workman uses it to conceal his malpractices. It is only when one turns over a Wilson jewel and looks at it from the back that the cunning and sweet reasonableness of the design become truly apparent. The soft 18-carat gold is often thinner than tin plate but channelled and flanged so as to give it a sufficiency of structural strength, for gold is not only valuable, but also heavy and for both reasons must be used sparingly. The Greeks and Etruscans made some of the finest jewels in history and yet their large collars and diadems weigh no more than a few penny-weights. Even the enamel on Wilson's jewels was used so that it would strengthen them (Colour Plate Vb).

It is often the jeweller's practice to use any odds and ends of contaminated enamel for the technically necessary layer of counter-enamelling at the back of a piece. Wilson on the other hand selected his counter enamels with care and fired them to crystal brightness. Even when the settings of the gems were buried deep in the design he enamelled them with scrupulous care.

Wilson would usually cover a joint between two pieces of metal with a tiny gold disc or a cluster of grains, not only to strengthen it, but because it looked good. His early training as an architect can easily be deduced from the logic of his designs, not only from the way in which the stresses and strains are distributed, but by the way in which structural necessity is made into aesthetic virtue. Wilson's book on silversmithing and jewellery remains a classic of what a technical manual should be and the advice it contains is as valid now as it was when it was published over seventy years ago.

John Paul Cooper was a colleague of Wilson's in the office of J. D. Seddings and remained to complete his articles when Wilson took over the practice. He too developed an interest in metalwork and started exhibiting at the Arts and Crafts Exhibition Society in 1894, although he was mainly concerned with plaster and gesso work. In 1898 he seems to have almost entirely given up architecture for craft work and in 1900 began to take the working of precious metals seriously. He took lessons in jewellery from John Innocent and Luigi Movio and in silversmithing from Lorenzo Colarossi, all of them Wilson's craftsmen. In 1901 he became head of the metalwork department at the Birmingham School of Art and in December of the same year he married his second cousin May Oliver. He gave up the appointment in Birmingham in 1907 and devoted himself to the making of jewellery full time.

There are many points of similarity between the work of Wilson and Cooper. Both had the same talent for sound engineering and often used the same tricks to achieve it—rondels and granules to reinforce the joints for example. Wilson's designs seem, however, to have welled out of his own inventiveness while Cooper was more receptive to influences from outside.

There had been some interest in Indian jewellery ever since the eighteen-eighties, but Cooper was one of the few jewellers who was prepared to learn real practical lessons from it. A belt which he made in 1905 is of W-shaped links fitting snugly together in a herringbone pattern and closely resembling the silverwork of primitive Dravidian tribesman, and a pearl and gold necklace which he made for his sister shows a decided Burmese influence.

The Japanese had a great influence on the Western craftsman, especially in the fields of metalwork and ceramics. Henry Wilson included in his book a supplement on Japanese metalworking techniques and his disciple Cooper made some use of the mokume technique in which three sheets of different metals are laminated together by soldering. The metal is then dented up from the back and the resulting bulge filed down flush to its surroundings so that concentric rings of contrasting coloured metal are exposed. Cooper does not always handle mokume with complete confidence and sometimes when he uses it to represent the markings on an insect or plant it appears so unemphatic as to matter little whether it is there or not. Sometimes he uses a combination of silver and copper with great success—in a border, for example, where it emphasizes the design without overstating it.

Cooper shares with Wilson a predilection for castles, towers, and citadels and ancient walled cities; indeed the holy city, the New Jerusalem, is very much a part of early twentieth-century symbolism.

Among the prettiest of his jewels are those little pendants which, within the agreeably random outlines of a seaside pebble, depict simple, almost naive subjects; a fat infant Moses cradled in a water-lily bloom enamelled to a faded pink, or a silver cupid cupped in the hollow of his own wings and perched upon a chrysoprase navette.

Arts and Crafts

THE GUILDS

The Arts and Crafts men were inveterate founders and joiners of guilds. It was almost as though they looked to them for mutual assurance that their perverse and difficult path was the true one; as though, like the monks of a closed order, they were seeking to exclude the corrupting influences of the twentieth century.

The Guild of Handicrafts, under the paternal leadership of *C.R. Ashbee* (1863–1942), was a microcosm of the whole Arts and Crafts scene with all its aspirations and tribulations. An architect by training and a socialist idealist in the true Morris mould, Ashbee founded the Guild and School of Handicrafts in 1888. The guild was to be a brotherhood of different craftsmen—carpenters, blacksmiths, jewellers, silversmiths and enamellers all working under one roof, carrying out their own designs and coming into direct contact with the customers.

At first, the little band of craftsmen in the East End workshops were modestly successful and it became quite chic to own their handcrafted furniture, table-silver and jewellery. In these early days orthodox experience in the trade was counted a drawback rather than an advantage. The workshop notes of Benvenuto Cellini were Ashbee's bible and he himself translated them into English and had them printed at Toynbee House.

Like Ruskin and Morris, Ashbee believed that the salvation of twentieth-century man was not to be found in the city and if the craftsman was to be the anchorman of the new society he must have his feet firmly planted on good English ploughland. In 1902 the lease on Essex House in the Mile End Road, home of the guild for the previous eleven years, expired. Once again Ashbee decided to put his ideas into practice. The guild, a community of 150 souls was uprooted and settled in the heart of the country, in Chipping Campden, a quiet Cotswold town untouched by the grimy hand of the Industrial Revolution.

Undoubtedly the move contributed to the disaster which was ultimately to overtake the guild. Rail costs to the great urban centres upon which, in spite of everything, they still found themselves dependent were a burden, particularly to London where they still had to maintain two retail outlets. Ashbee does not seem to have formed a significant clientele among the local landowners who should have been his new patrons, the fault, possibly, of his own personality. In hard times, in the old Mile End Road days, it had been the custom for the older guildsmen to stand down and take temporary jobs in the East End factories and workshops. This could not work in Chipping Campden where there was no alternative employment for them to go to. And hard times, in the form of the 1905 depression, were just around the corner.

Competition was a growing problem, not only from the mighty industrial dragon against which they had unsheathed the sword in the first place. The attack was on both flanks, a double threat which Ashbee caricatured as 'dear Emily' and 'Messrs Nobody and Nowhere'. The latter were the big firms: Ashbee complained that they stole his designs wholesale, and certainly the best of them were very successful at adapting the Arts and Crafts idiom to mass production and produced jewellery which was attractive in both design and price.

'Dear Emily' was the amateur, usually a young lady with time on her hands and father's money to subsidize her, who turned her hand to jewellery and enamelling. Arts and Crafts had become as fashionable as drawing, needlework and poetry had once been. Dear Emily could afford to cost out her work at tuppence an hour whilst the craftsman had to charge a shilling. Sadly this was often all her time was worth. Nonetheless, Ashbee had a soft spot for her and in return for a fee of a pound a week allowed her to invade his workshop and pester his craftsmen so that she could learn the right way of doing things. Ashbee was an amateur himself in the pure sense of loving what he was doing and this was the quality which appealed to him in dear Emily.

Before the move the guild had been made a limited company which increased the cost of administration and the ultimate price of the product. But it was the trade depression of 1905 which sounded the death knell of the guild which went into voluntary liquidation in 1907, although Ashbee himself remained in Chipping Campden until 1919.

Many of the jewel designs were from the hand of Ashbee himself, others were by W. A. White. The 'poor peacock' motif seems to have had great personal significance for Ashbee and the bird appears in several of the guild's jewels (Plate 47). 'The craft of the guild', a trim little sailing galley, was another favourite design. A necklace designed by White in the Victoria and Albert Museum uses simple enamels set in light mounts, like gems, together with white opals (Plate 48).

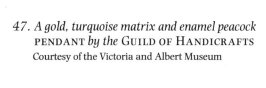

47. A gold, turquoise matrix and enamel peacock
PENDANT *by the* GUILD OF HANDICRAFTS
Courtesy of the Victoria and Albert Museum

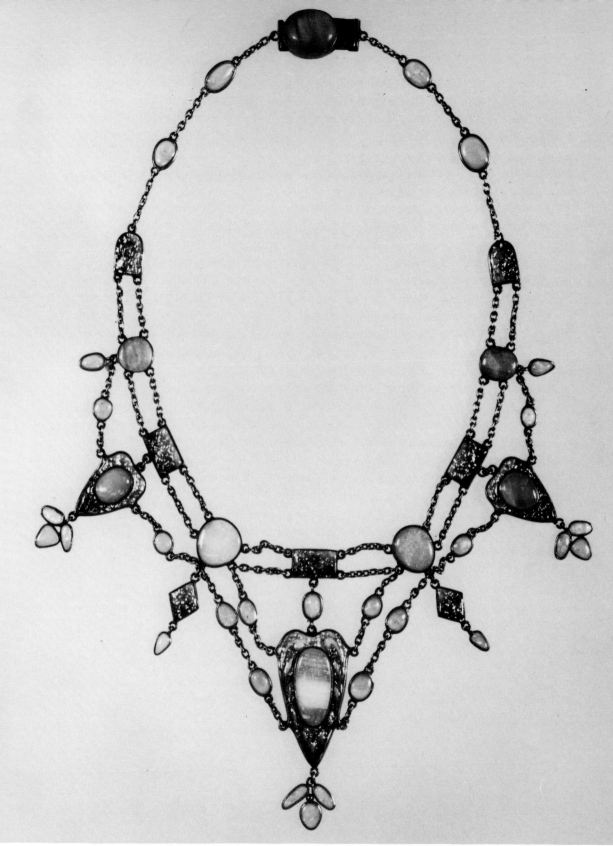

48. An opal and enamel NECKLACE *by the* GUILD OF HANDICRAFTS

The Artificers' Guild was founded by Nelson Dawson in 1901. Montagu Fordham took it over in 1903 and established it at 9 Maddox Street, London W1 where it continued to operate until the First World War. Edward Spencer was the guild's chief designer and he appears to have gone in for jewels of a heavily allegorical nature. The Ariadne necklace, the design of which was shared by Spencer with John Houghton Bonner, was very typical of the Artificers' style (Plate 49).

Guilds sprang up all over the British Isles: there were guilds in Birmingham, Bromsgrove, Barnstaple and Edinburgh and the hardened guildsman went from one to another. *Fred Partridge*, the son of a Barnstaple chemist was apprenticed at Chipping Campden for two years from 1902. From there he went back to his home town to work with the Barnstaple guild of metalworkers.

Partridge appears to have been open to every kind of influence: his pins and pendants with cruciform designs and high-domed and toothed collets suggest French and Flemish peasant jewellery; his horn back-hair combs, in spite of a certain British stiffness and a native gothic up-and-down quality, owe a great deal to Lalique; and his belt buckles and girdles in their formalism and angularity have a great deal of Glasgow and Vienna about them. The round brooches look as though they might have been derived from the Anglo-Saxon saucer brooch. Partridge was an excellent craftsman who experimented widely in different materials and at various times made use of brass, copper, steel, horn and shell in his work as well as the orthodox precious stones and metals.

In 1903 he married May Hart, an accomplished enamellist, who was later to teach at Sir John Cass. Before 1914 he had a shop in Dean Street, but during the Great War he was on munition work. Peace found him at Ditchling, the informal craft community founded by Eric Gill, a familiar figure in a shaggy Norwegian jersey.

LIBERTY'S

Many commercial firms began to capitalize on the popularity of Arts and Crafts designs by mass producing them mechanically, and none of them with more taste and success than Liberty. Arthur Lazenby Liberty was a draper by trade and when in 1875 he opened his shop at 218 Regent Street his intention was to import and retail oriental silks and fabrics. He chose exactly the right moment, for the aesthetic movement which cherished a passion for anything oriental was just taking off.

The enterprise was an immediate success and Liberty's gorgeous displays of oriental fabrics and works of art drew the intelligentsia of the day like bees to a honeypot; Carlisle, Ruskin, the Rossettis, Burne Jones and Morris were frequent visitors. In 1899 it was decided to manufacture a range of jewels and domestic silver.

Arts and Crafts

The best modern designers were to be engaged and the jewels were to be marketed under the name 'Cymric'.

Some of the work was done in London but most was carried out in Birmingham at the works of W. H. Haseler. In 1901 a new company was formed, Liberty and Co. (Cymric), to which Haseler's sold most of their plant and premises in return for two thousand pounds worth of shares. By this excellent arrangement not only could Haseler's pursue their own work, but they were also able to mark and market some Liberty designs as their own. The latter were marked W.H.H.

Some of the brightest talents of the day were employed on the Cymric collection, and although Liberty's insisted on absolute anonymity it is known that Bernard Cuzner, Jessie King, A. H. Jones and Arthur Gaskin contributed designs to it. The jewels, although stamped out mechanically, were finished by hand and this lip service to the Arts and Crafts ideal was probably one of the reasons why they were such a commercial success. It must be said, though, that when the hand finishing involved saw-piercing this could be so perfunctory that it would have been better for it to have been cleanly punched with a machine. Elements of the jewel were often beaten with a hammer to give an interesting texture. In a hand-made piece this was a natural part of the craft process whereas Liberty used it to disguise the agency of the machine.

The precious stones are rarely to be seen in Liberty's jewels, but turquoise matrix, blister pearls, tourmalines, amethysts and especially moonstones, semi-precious gems worth at that time no more than a few coppers a carat, were extensively and intelligently used. The traditional way of setting a cabochon stone is in a little collar soldered to the surface of the piece. The edge of this is then rubbed down over the circumference of the gem to hold it in. Settings of this kind can easily be produced in quantity for use with stones of standard dimensions and Liberty employed them in many designs. Some jewels, however, were designed to be set with gems in random shapes and sizes and here the gem was poked through the setting from the back and there secured with a lip of metal. Naturally the aperture had to be smaller than the gem and the edges of it were always turned upwards so that the setting was faired into the stone. The effect is very good and suits these designs perfectly.

Many of the Cymric designs were from the hand of *Archibald Knox* (1864–1933), a Manxman. Trained at Douglas School of Art he came south in 1897 to lecture at three of the Surrey art schools. He was working for Liberty around 1905 and returned to the Isle of Man in 1912. Knox's work owes something to Early Celtic designs with their serpentine curves and intricate interlacements. One of his favourite motifs resembles a triangle with its corners attenuated into wave scrolls like an ideograph for a sailing boat in some obscure calligraphy (Plate 50). Neatly stylized birds are a feature of his designs. *Oliver Baker* (1859–1939) also designed for

49. *The Ariadne* NECKLACE: *a gold, silver, enamel and diamond collar designed by* EDWARD SPENCER *and* JOHN BONNER. *The gold figure of Ariadne stands at the centre of the pendant embowered in vines with the sea at her feet and the starry crown of her immortality above her. Medallions of Eros and Anteros hang at each side. The chain represents the cities of the Cretan king and of the father of Theseus together with the galleys of the Cretan fleet, linked by sprays of ivy, fig and ilex and chains of sea shells and fir cones*

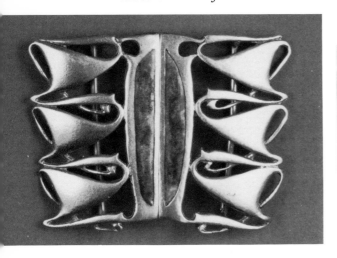

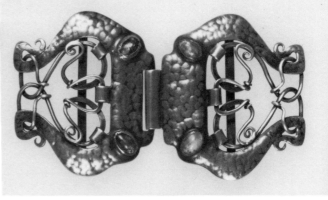

50. *A silver and enamel* BELT CLASP *designed by* ARCHIBALD KNOX *for Liberty and Co.*

51. *A silver and turquoise matrix* BELT CLASP *designed by* OLIVER LAKER *for Liberty and Co.*

Liberty: clasps by him contrast thick, succulent vegetal motifs with lithe, nervously coiling scrolls (Plate 51).

The range and variety of the jewels which Liberty made is in itself impressive, from simple, modest pieces in silver and semi-precious stones to quite elaborate ornaments in exquisitely inlaid opal and 18-carat gold (Plate 52, Colour Plate XIa). The firm also imported jewellery for sale: traditional Indian jewels, art nouveau pieces from Paris and jugendstil jewels from Pforzheim.

GLASGOW AND THE SCOTS

It would be impossible to exaggerate the influence which the Glasgow style had upon European decorative art in the twentieth century. It was a style whose very essence was paradox, which was more Scottish than British and more European than either, a microcosm of early twentieth-century decorative art, which embodied before 1900 not only the distortions, sinuosities and grotesque phantasy of Parisian art nouveau, but also the powerful geometry of Vienna and Berlin which was eventually to lay art nouveau to rest.

At the time the little band of Glasgow designers were largely ignored or at most contemptuously dismissed as 'the spook school'. In 1907 the *Art Journal* cited Glasgow as far less important than Edinburgh and Aberdeen and then quoted the names of some now forgotten artists without even mentioning the famous 'Four': the

Macdonald sisters, Herbert MacNair and above all, Charles Rennie Mackintosh who we recognize today as the fountainhead of twentieth-century design in the decorative arts. Mackintosh was so much the leading light of the Glasgow school and the movement was so closely linked with his personality and style that the others, particularly the brilliant Macdonald girls, are often overlooked.

Mackintosh was trained as an architect and he is best remembered for the buildings and interiors which he designed, particularly the Glasgow School of Art which caused such a furore at the time and which today still has the power to take our breath away for its originality and sheer modernity. Although he did not make a lot of jewellery his influence on design was deep and continuing.

Typical of Mackintosh are the undecorated verticals and oddly stylized female figures holding vast cabbage roses—the forerunners of the 'sausage roll roses' which were to be such a feature of art deco design a decade later. As one of his contemporaries remarked in 1897: 'Certain conventional distortions, harpies, mermaids, cariatids and the rest are accepted why should a worker today not make patterns out of people if he pleases?'[6] In Paris Lalique was presenting the same

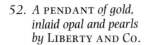

52. A PENDANT *of gold,
inlaid opal and pearls
by* LIBERTY AND CO.

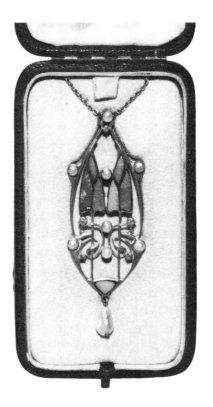

6. *Studio*, July 1897.

challenge to the established conventions of the age by adapting the human figure to the purposes of his designs.

It would be wrong, though, to try and establish a link between Glasgow and Paris on such evidence, for on the face of it Mackintosh was quite out of sympathy with French art nouveau. As Mrs May Sturrock recollected: 'Mackintosh didn't like art nouveau, he fought against it with these straight lines against these things you can see for yourself are like melted margarine or slightly deliquescent lard.'[7]

It was perhaps this struggle between order and anarchy, leaping energy versus languid decay which is the secret common to both French art nouveau and the Glasgow designers. The art nouveau whip-scroll is not really amorphous, it is struggling against a brute geometric discipline which tugs it into sharply angled returns and sudden horizontals. Similarly, the strange anthropomorphic creatures of the Four struggle to be mortal against the awful linear spell. The motive force behind English Arts and Crafts was different—there the essential tensions were between the craftsman and his medium, the design and the materials.

The Four were so closely linked by ties of friendship and marriage that it was not possible to say that one particular style or motif was the exclusive property of any one of them. In Glasgow the cross pollination of ideas was just as important as it was in London or Birmingham.

Herbert MacNair (1868–1955) was apprenticed to architecture and by a happy chance found himself working side by side with Mackintosh in the same office. Illustrations of his work suggest an interesting effect which he seems to have achieved with silver wire, bunching it together in coils and skeins and then using it as a frame or border. He seems to have used overlays of wire too, fusing random strands of it to a relief so that the plump figures of children seem to be playing hide and seek in a briar thicket. Strange little not-quite-human faces peer from some of his jewels sheathed in leaf-like cowls, and it is interesting to note that similar motifs appear on the now famous poster for the Scottish Musical Review designed by Mackintosh. In 1899 MacNair married Frances Macdonald.

In spite of their family name the *Macdonald sisters*[8] were English by birth but moved to Scotland in their teens. The girls were known to have been at Glasgow Art School in 1891 where they were studying freehand drawing, model drawing, ornament, anatomy and plant drawing. After graduating the sisters opened a studio in the city for the decorative arts. Their work has a fey, unearthly quality which is never coy or cute but often sinister, even repellent yet with a luminous, other worldly feeling. The same mood can be sensed in the stories of Stevenson and Barrie.

7. *Connoisseur*, August 1973, 'Remembering Charles Rennie Mackintosh', a recorded interview with Mrs May Sturrock, June Bedford and Ivor Driver.
8. Frances (1874–1921), Margaret (1865–1933).

The fairies of the Macdonald sisters are not to be found at the bottom of any suburban garden but are the insomniac creatures of the dank glen, the still pond and the heaving burial mound. A silver comb by Frances shows two confronted female faces above a paired-heart motif wound with strands of flowering briar, and the long tresses of the women form the teeth of the comb. The same motifs occur in a pendant by Margaret; the heads wear close-fitting helmets and face one another atop of tall stems—plant women in fact. The jewel, in silver, rubies, pearls and turquoises, is as slim and vertical as an icicle and the heart motif hangs below it from an immensely long chain. The effect is bizarre to the point of being disturbing and shows how much the Four had in common. Mackintosh and Margaret Macdonald were married in 1900.

There were others too, who although outside the enchanted circle of the Four were yet closely identified with it. *Talwyn Morris* (1865–1911) was another English emigré. Originally destined for the church he too was articled to an architect, his uncle Joseph Morris of Reading. Eventually he became art director of *Black and White* magazine and then moved to Glasgow to become art director of Blackie's, the publishers.

Morris specialized in repoussé work which shows all the angularities and perpendicularities which one has come to expect from the Glasgow school. Bird motifs occur in his work, especially owls, often just the creature's heart-shaped mask, highly stylized and with precious stones for eyes. He worked not only in silver, but also in copper and aluminium.

Jessie M. King (1875–1949), the brilliant book illustrator, also worked in jewellery. Her father, the Reverend James King, discouraged her from any art work so she had to confine her activities to school hours and hide her drawings in the hedge in case her mother should find them and tear them up. She would draw pictures in pipeclay on any convenient stone—indeed as an old lady in Kirkudbright she is remembered for drawing landscapes on her doorstep like this.

At last Dr King relented and allowed her to enrol as a full-time student at Glasgow Art School where she soon came under the benign influence of the principal Francis Newberry, 'that tycoon of art education' as Robert Furneaux Jordan called him. Of her jewellery she is well known for the buckles which she designed for Liberty. Here the influence of Mackintosh is very apparent, for the bird motifs on the buckle (Plate 53) also appear on the Scottish Musical Review poster.

The Glasgow school were very much a minority among Scottish craftsmen who for the most part worked in the style of Birmingham, South Kensington or Chipping Campden, producing jewellery which although unmistakably British was not specifically Scottish.

Phoebe Traquair (1852–1936), worked in Edinburgh though like many enamellists

53. Silver and enamel BUCKLE *designed by* JESSIE M. KING *for Liberty and Co.*

of her day she seems to have been influenced by Fisher. Her enamels often depict a vaguely allegorical subject like 'Earthspun' or 'Out of the deep' (Colour Plate XIb). Her work is sure and sensitive, the colours luminous and skilfully heightened with paillons of bright foil embedded in the enamel. Faintly opalescent, the faces of her nymphs and fairies look as creatures of the underworld ought to look, earthy and alien. The painted enamels are fired on copper, the reverse usually counter-enamelled in clear colourless flux with the title and date of the work lettered in (Colour Plate VIIa).

James Cromer Watts was established in Aberdeen and took seventeenth- and eighteenth-century Iberian jewellery for his inspiration with varying success. The *lazo* or ribbon-bow brooch of Spanish peasant regalia is known to have been imitated by him and so were the dragon pendants of the Spanish renaissance. The pendant illustrated is of a similar kind, but probably more Italian than Spanish in affinity (Plate 54). James Cromer Watts could portray the female figure with considerable skill and fluency, and this was perhaps the best of his work.

72

ART NOUVEAU AND ARTS AND CRAFTS

Any comparison between Arts and Crafts and art nouveau is notable more for its differences than its similarities. Nevertheless, it would be impossible for two such vital movements to coexist without coming into contact, however fleetingly. It has even been suggested that art nouveau had some roots in early Arts and Crafts and certainly the jewel designs of *Sir Alfred Gilbert* (1854–1934) could conceivably have had an influence. Gilbert was always well ahead of his time, and those pieces which he improvised himself out of swiftly bent and twisted wire would not have seemed out of place in the 1960s.

There is something of Gilbert's spontaneity and vigour in the jewels of *Alfred Jones*, a pupil at Vittoria Street: more than a suggestion of art nouveau too in these complex designs of enlaced tendrils and scrolls, tapered and tipped with droplets of gold (Colour Plate XIc). Sometimes, though, structural weaknesses mar his work and the different elements of the design do not seem to support and buttress one another as they ought.

54. *A* PENDANT *in gold, opal, pearl and blue enamel by* JAMES CROMER WATTS *of Aberdeen*

55. *Carved ivory, silver and mother-of-pearl* BROOCH *by*
A. C. JAHN

The jewels of *A. C. Jahn*, although they lack the langour and oversubtlety of art nouveau are clearly in this style. Like Wolfers in Brussels, Jahn used carved ivory in his work and there are other similarities, not so much of technique as of mood and feeling. Jahn was another art-school man and principal of the Municipal School of Art in Wolverhampton. He used colour with unobtrusive skill, the buttery pallor of ivory, the dark glimmer of smoked shell, the blues, browns and golds of oxidized silver with bright parcel-gilding for contrast and emphasis (Plate 55).

Whatever the origins of art nouveau, it developed quite differently from Arts and Crafts. Far from rejecting the orthodox jewellery trade, men like Lalique, Boucheron and Vever were not only an avant-garde, but a revered élite, whose families in some cases had been practising jewellers for generations. There was no question as to the way in which they acquired their knowledge, for it was already at their finger tips, often as the result of a long and exacting formal apprenticeship. They were not concerned about elevating the status of the craftsman for the French already regarded him as an artist in his own right.

74

The French jeweller was a professional, who did not mix his politics with his métier, and revolution and its disastrous effects on the luxury trades were no stranger to him. With true Gallic pragmatism he recognized that he depended for his livelihood on the continuation of a wealthy privileged class and he had no wish to kill the goose that laid the golden egg.

Although some craftsmen like Ramsden, Cooper, Wilson and Stabler were still at work after the First World War, the driving force of Arts and Crafts had wound down by 1914. Even without the war and the social changes which it set in motion, Arts and Crafts, by its very nature and the philosophy which motivated it could not have survived for much longer. The movement erected around itself a hothouse to protect it from the boisterous winds of twentieth-century reality and like all such growths it flourished for a time with unnatural vigour and just as swiftly withered away.

The most brash and ill-advised assumption of Arts and Crafts was that it had nothing to learn from the jewellery trade. It had everything to learn, and indeed something to teach it, but with a pig-headedness tinged with the heroic the Arts and Crafts men brushed aside firsthand knowledge from tradesmen who, whether they liked it or not, were the heirs to half a millenium of accumulated experience. The ancient traditions of the jeweller may have been dormant in some instances but they still existed, unbroken and very much alive. Arts and Crafts workers still chose to do it the hard way, making breathtaking discoveries which were commonplace to every apprentice, scouring ancient treatises for knowledge of techniques which were still in daily use.

They turned away from everything the contemporary jeweller did best: saw-piercing and pavé-setting were rejected as though they were some obscure form of sexual deviation—in fact their whole attitude had that obsessive priggishness of the more extreme religious sects, equating technical skill with the allurements of the scarlet woman. Arthur Lazenby Liberty described the French art nouveau jewels in the Budapest exhibition of 1906 as 'erotic imaginings of morbid brains depicted with a technical mastery only too wickedly perfect'.

That jewellery is not only an art but also a luxury the Arts and Crafts people had to discover for themselves. Inevitably they found out that they were dependent for customers on the very class that as socialists they were pledged to abolish and the trade depression of 1905 must have hastened that discovery.

The isolation of Arts and Crafts was almost complete. They indignantly rejected the 'art for art's sake' of the aesthete only to replace it with their own 'craft for craft's sake'. The best of them trudged a circular path that began with them studying in the art schools and ended with them teaching there. Few, if any of the legions whose work was so praised in the pages of *The Studio* went to work in trade workshops, the melancholy truth being that only a handful of them ever achieved sufficient technical skill.

Eventually this feverish enthusiasm untempered by contact with real life consumed itself like a dragon eating its own tail. Perhaps the real problem was that society was not ready for Arts and Crafts and that it was seventy years before its time.

4 · The Twenties

Everything which typifies twenties fashion for us—the tango, the tassels, the slender Poiret dress line, the ardent biting colours were all on the scene well before 1914. There was one sad casualty of the war though: too subdued and well mannered to survive in the noisy post-war world the swags and garlands of the neo-classical style were soon to disappear almost without trace.

EARRINGS

Earrings were not only still fashionable but the austere new bobbed and shingled hair styles required that they be bigger and brasher than they had been for half a century—by 1929 they were almost touching the shoulder. The dress line was of gothic perpendicularity, the waist dragged down to mid-hip where it was often accentuated with a brooch on one side. Long earrings not only reinforced this emphasis on the vertical but had other uses too: the short hair styles no longer flattered or concealed a too powerful jawline to which the distraction of a pair of earrings could be a godsend.

The Afro-American influences which were so apparent in popular music and the arts may have had something to do with the craze for Creole earrings. The large pendulous rings of these Creole styles did not have to be of metal and were just as often carved *en bloc* from semi-precious stone, bevelled or faceted circles of crystal, onyx, cornelian or apple-green dyed chalcedony, or the flat annuli of jade which the Chinese prize so highly. The firm of Charles Packer marketed a Creole earring with three interchangeable drops—faceted rings of onyx, crystal or cornelian which could be selected by the wearer according to her fancy. If anything, this kind of gimmick was even more popular with the twenties flapper than it had been with her Victorian mother.

The choice in earring designs was enormous: briolettes of crystal, torpedoes of amber or cornelian (Plate 56), slim lance-like diamond drops articulated as cunningly as the shell of a prawn (Plate 57). Onyx drops were hung in tandem, two

57. Diamond drop EARRINGS *of a design which originated just before the First World War*

56. Cornelian, onyx and diamond EARRINGS

58. Onyx and diamond EARRINGS

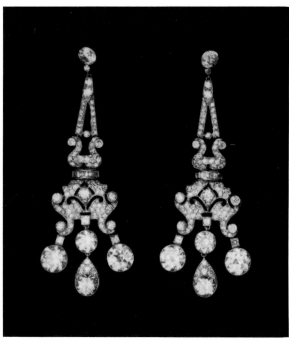

59. Pagoda-shaped pearl, rose-diamond, onyx and coral EARRINGS

60. A pair of diamond girandole EARRINGS decorated with lily motifs

from each ear so that one swung slightly lower than the other, an echo of the Edwardian négligé (Plate 58). There were pearl and diamond tassels and fringes (Plate 59) and big diamond girandoles (Plate 60). Chinese jade was in great demand and wafer thin panels of it carved with traditional songbirds and sacred mushrooms, bats and gourds were delicately hung from the lobe of the ear by thin chains of diamonds and platinum. In spite of this diversity most earrings were of the pendent variety and it was not until the thirties that the more compact earstud came to be worn. As a rule simpler designs date from just after the war and the larger and more exuberant styles were worn between 1926 and 1929.

NECKLETS AND SAUTOIRS

Négligés and la Vallières survived almost into the thirties. Most of the changes had already been rung on these styles by 1914 and it is impossible to say, simply by looking at one of these jewels, whether it was made before or after the war.

The tassels which Paul Poiret had introduced before 1914 were even more in evidence now. Strands of seed pearls were twisted into long ropes as thick as a finger and worn slung round the neck like a scarf, the dangling ends finished off with tassels. Tassels could be so closely linked to costume in materials as well as design that they could scarcely be called jewellery at all: silk tassels formed pendants to long sautoirs of the same material tied into decorative knots. Sautoirs of moiré silk ribbon had rows of a dozen or so real or imitation beads at each side and were finished off with a tassel in the front. Rows upon rows of swaying, clicking beads were one of the almost inevitable hallmarks of the twenties flapper—another style which harks back to the early years of the century. It is this quality of movement which so many of the jewels of the twenties have in common. The Western world had gone dance-mad and its jewels were expressly created to sway and clash to the lunatic footwork of the Charleston and the Black Bottom.

When a woman spent so many of the nocturnal hours in the fickle embraces of the dance floor her back was the only part of her body she could effectively expose. Her neckline at the rear dived almost to the sacro-iliac, and the focal point of the necklace moved round to the back in sympathy so that the pendant was often suspended here rather than between the breasts. Sometimes, too, choker collars of large beads were fastened at the back, not with a neat and unobtrusive clasp, but with a bow of black velvet, a fashion probably suggested by eighteenth-century portraits.

The Twenties

BANGLES AND BRACELETS

Slave bangles were as popular as ever, changing only in their secondary function. Long gloves were less often worn, but the slave bangle was invaluable in camouflaging the vaccination scar which so many of the young now carried on their upper arm. The choice was as varied as ever—bamboo, plain, engine-turned or faceted. One design like two lance-corporal's chevrons joined tip to tip was called the 'merrythought' from its tenuous resemblance to the lucky wishbone, another was of woven gold in the form of a coiled serpent. More luxurious versions of the slave bangle came set with a row of diamond brilliants, calibré-cut onyx or coloured stones, often in suites of three. Bracelets of mesh-like Milanese chain were provided with an adjustable clasp so that they could be worn anywhere on the arm. Decoration was either woven into the mesh in a contrasted coloured gold, or stamped into it.

At first bracelets were slender, often no more than a single row of small stones set in box collets—platinum for diamonds and gold for coloured stones—and so cunningly and invisibly linked as to be as supple as a piece of string. Other designs used links of carved cornelian, onyx or dyed agate (Colour Plate XIVa). Towards 1929 they grew progressively more massive, their big square links often ballasted with cabochon gems (Plate 86). The tango bracelet, retailed by Harrods at five pounds, had big studs of lapis lazuli connected by shuttle-shaped links of engine-turned gold. These big bracelets of the late twenties were not meant to be worn singly. According to the *Goldsmiths Journal* in 1928, 'bracelets by the armful is still the Paris rule' and the rule it was to remain for several years to come on both sides of the channel.

Nancy Cunard epitomized this barbaric fashion. Her slender figure was cast in the Van Dongen mould, swathed in silk or the pelts of savage beasts and 'her fine boned arms both encased in such a concatenation of weighty armlets of rigid African ivory that the least movement produced a clacking sound as of billiard balls or the cakewalk of a skeleton'.[1] Nancy Cunard's bracelets were African fighting bracelets, the massive rings of ivory used in tribal warfare. Occasionally, in moments of exasperation, she recalled them to their original purpose by tearing them off and pelting her long-suffering friend Henry Crowder, the pianist, with them.

1. Daphne Fielding, *Emerald and Nancy, Lady Cunard and her Daughter*, 1968.

61. A diamond BANDEAU

BANDEAUX AND HAIR ORNAMENTS

For the head, the bandeau was even more popular than it had been pre-war and was worn either on the hair-line or well back like a halo (Plate 61). There was a variety of clips and slides for the hair: favourites were: a diamond arrow, a simple annulus of pavé-set stones or paste, or a pair of tortoiseshell prongs with horseshoe-shaped heads. All of these styles had an Edwardian pedigree.

Laura Corrigan, the American society hostess was noted for wearing a brilliant auburn wig—in fact several wigs, including one casually dishevelled for country weekends and another with attached bathing cap for swimming. When she asked Emerald, Lady Cunard whether she was going to wear a tiara for a gala night at the opera that lady was heard to reply, 'No dear, just a small emerald bandeau and my own hair.' The lavish parties with which Laura attempted to take London society by storm were a legend, as were the gifts and prizes which she distributed at them with the careless munificence of a caliph—coroneted sock suspenders for dukes, braces with 18-carat gold fittings by Cartier for lesser mortals.

PINS AND BROOCHES

Although the idea of the sûreté pin germinated well before 1914, it did not really come into its own until the twenties. The basic pin had a fixed decorative motif at the

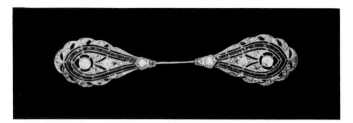

62. A diamond and calibré-cut sapphire SÛRETÉ -PIN

head and another clipped over the point. The latter could be removed to enable the point to be skewered through the clothing and then replaced to prevent it from slipping out. At first they were called veil pins, hat brooches or arrow brooches, and one of the most popular designs was indeed that of the arrow, the head being the removable part. Sûreté pins came in various sizes up to four inches in length. The smallest were used to fasten motoring veils. Sometimes the ends of the pin were unmatched—of different size and different design. One such, sold by Mappin and Webb, had a ring of frosted crystal at one end and a pavé-set diamond motif at the other. For the sporting there was a small pin of the veil-fastener type with a rose-diamond retriever and a game bird. Of the equal-ended sûreté pins many must have been made into pairs of earrings into which they could easily be adapted. The favourite designs were of lotus buds, papyrus and palmettes, often set with diamonds, black onyx or pearls, occasionally with a few calibré-cut coloured stones (Plate 62).

In spite of the persistence of many Edwardian styles there was much that was new in the twenties. Around 1925 a special brooch was devised to be worn in the deep

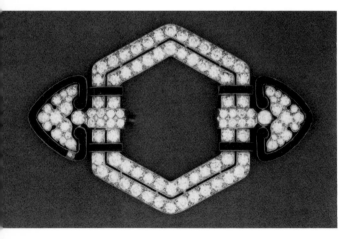

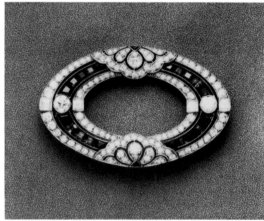

63. A diamond and calibré-cut onyx HAT BROOCH

64. A diamond and calibré-cut sapphire HAT BROOCH

82

65. (above) *A sapphire, diamond and carved-crystal* HAT BROOCH

66. (right) *Paste monkey* BROOCH, *a design which originated before 1914*

cloche hats of the day. Most of these hat brooches were variations on the theme of an open-centred oblong: an oval link of polished onyx held between diamond palmettes; an open-centred shuttle motif set with pearls, sapphires or diamonds; or less typically a ring of frosted crystal between diamond-set ribbon tails (Plates 63, 64, 65).

Among the most charming jewels of the twenties were those brooches, usually of modest size, representing a pot of growing flowers. Although unconnected with the pre-war Louis Seize style these designs clearly originated in the *giardinetto* jewels of the eighteenth century. Typical would be a shallow *tazza* of onyx and diamonds overflowing with leaves and flowers of carved emeralds, sapphires and rubies. These stones, shaped by Indian lapidaries occur time and again in the jewels of the twenties and thirties and must have been shipped to Europe in some quantity.

NOVELTIES

Novelties like the acrobatic monkeys were still going strong (Plate 66). The Pip, Squeak and Wilfred charm was right up to the minute though and represented the dog-rabbit-penguin trio of the *Daily Mirror* comic strip. Dog brooches continued to grow in popularity until the 1940s. Chicks were still firm favourites, so were owls. The 'lucky owl' brooch with the bird perched on a new moon cost £1 12s 6d from Charles Packer. Lingerie clips were sold in sets of four, flat bands of gold designed to keep the shoulder straps of the camisole in place. These little jewels were very simply decorated with no more than a little saw-piercing or a minute cabochon sapphire, turquoise or pearl.

Typical of the gimmickry of this time were those jewels which could be converted or split up into other quite different jewels. 'Parts of a necklace will unscrew to make earrings (according to whether you are wearing your morning shingle or your evening chignon). Another part can be detached to make a brooch.' The necklace of 1929 often formed two or more bracelets.

CRAFT JEWELLERS

What remained of Arts and Crafts survived only as an anachronism in the hustling cynical twenties. It had acquired by this time a rather seedy suburban image of corduroys and sandals and nut cutlets. Some workshops doggedly survived the war to continue much as they had done before—Cooper, Wilson and Ramsden. Other craftsmen like Murphy and Stabler changed direction to make a significant contribution to British art deco—although they seem to have inclined more towards silversmithing.

Henry George Murphy (1884–1939) was an apprentice of Henry Wilson in the nineties. In 1912 he was working with Emil Lettre in Berlin and he set up his London workshop in the following year. Murphy's influence was powerful and benevolent. He taught at the Royal College of Arts and the Central, of which he became principal in 1937. Murphy had a fine sense of colour and handled enamel with great skill and his art deco bears the unmistakable influence of the Ballet Russe.

Sybil Dunlop came of Scots parents who at the turn of the century sent her to school in Brussels to learn French, and it was here, at a time when it was lady-like to learn about making jewellery that she picked up the rudiments of her craft.

One of her main reasons for going into business was to provide a home and livelihood for her old nurse, and Nanny Frost was installed upstairs in the shop in Kensington Church Street where she looked after the books for many years.

It was an unusual shop: an immense copper lantern hung outside, and the four craftsmen worked within where customers could look over their shoulders and watch the work in progress. Miss Dunlop presided over it all, a dramatic figure costumed in an embroidered caftan and Russian boots.

W. Nathanson joined her right at the beginning in the early twenties, a lad of sixteen fresh from John Cass, and his contribution to the firm and the style which it evolved was a vital one. Today the designs usually associated with Sybil Dunlop are the stylized leaves and tight wire scrolls of the later Arts and Crafts movement. Nathanson rejects this 'leaf and bead work' as being early and untypical. For him the firm's highest achievement was the 'carpet of gems', mainly stained agate, opals and garnets, carefully cut to measure and set edge to edge in bold geometric patterns (Colour Plate XIIa). The stones were not cut on the premises, but by an Idar Oberstein lapidary firm. Two sets of brass gauges pierced with holes corresponding in size and shape to the gems used in the designs were held, one in Kensington, the other at the factory in Germany. Gems could then be ordered by number in the certainty that they would be of exactly the right dimensions. Moonstones were favoured in their jewels, so were fine fire opals which were brought to them yearly by two brothers from Idar who had acquired the concession to a mine in Mexico.

Nathanson would have no truck with arty-crafty prejudice. He made expert use of the piercing-saw and is firmly convinced that the reason why the Arts and Crafters were so set against it was that they lacked the necessary skill to use it. The firm's enamelling was done by a Belgian named de Konningh (who also worked for Ramsden), often in the Renaissance manner of black scrollwork flecked with white. The approach was an eclectic one and Celtic and Holbeinesque designs were used as well as the more familiar 'carpet of gems' and leaf and bead motifs. Designs were seldom repeated (Colour Plate XIIc).

When war broke out in 1939 the firm was disbanded. Nathanson served as a fireman throughout the London blitz, but Sybil's health broke down so irrecoverably that when peace came again she was unable to return to work. In spite of the crippling burden of post-war purchase tax Nathanson got the firm on its feet again and ran it until his retirement in 1971 when it was closed down.

SAH OVED

The most original and individual talent at work in Britain before the war was *Sah Oved*. Although trained in the Arts and Crafts tradition she was always her own woman going her own highly individual way. She had very little formal training and she has been a great believer in finding out for herself and getting on with it.

She first saw jewellery in the making at art school in Chichester and since then never wanted to do anything else. The Great War years were spent in medical research in Cambridge and evening classes learning to make jewellery alongside war-crippled ex-miners who were being taught the craft in the hope of finding them alternative employment.

The Twenties

She was with John Paul Cooper in 1923 and in 1927 began working with her partner, the extraordinary Moshe Oved. Oved was a Polish Jew who set out to become a rabbi but became a watch-maker instead. A brilliant showman he presided over Cameo Corner, his shop in Museum Street, gowned like an alchemist of old in an ankle-length caftan, practically giving away jewels and objects of virtu to those clients to whom he took a fancy and proportionately overcharging those with whom he felt less in sympathy.

In 1927 the Oveds moved to Jerusalem. The change was not a success. Many Jewish scholars were then living in the city and among them the high priest of Museum Street was 'just another eccentric Jew'. The couple moved back to London in 1937.

A nervous man of many phobias, marked both physically and mentally by the anti-semitism he grew up with, Moshe nevertheless chose to stay in London during the blitz. During one raid he was trembling so much that Sah gave him some modelling wax to steady his hands. The result was the first of a series of charming rings, each made like a little new-born animal, a lamb or a kid, its unsteady legs forming the shank.

What strikes one about Sah's work is that in spite of the variety of both design and technique, each piece comes unmistakably from the same sure and clever hand, the same playful but sensitive intellect. The gold is always 22-carat, peerless in colour, texture and plasticity, and many of her jewels bear exquisite engraved inscriptions: a necklace set with flashing mirrors of Vauxhall glass and dripping with topazes and peridots is inscribed 'Mirror Mirror on the Wall'. This literary and allegorical element in her work is never pompous or contrived but gives her jewels a special runic magic, the stuff that folk tales are made of. A winged lion of Judah bursts from the side of a big gold bracelet like an imprisoned djinn and this jewel also carries its inscription. In spite of being born a Christian—in fact her family heartily disapproved of her association with a Jewish shopkeeper—Jewish folklore is strong in her work. A cabochon sapphire in the bezel of a ring is buttressed by arcaded shoulders with roofs of gold tiles sheltering human figures so minute that she remembers having to wet her finger to pick them up from the bench. The affinity with a Jewish wedding ring here is very strong.

Sah Oved's jewellery embraces an extraordinary range of techniques, materials and emotions, for this is, perhaps above all, emotional jewellery—who can doubt the good humour of her 'sad ring' with its wistful agate faces, or the passion of the 'crown of thorns' necklace with its red raw coral and tranquil rosettes of carved mother-of-pearl (Colour Plate XIII).

GOLD MESH

The jewels of the twenties were still comparatively light both in setting and in design. Rayon, the new cellullose dress material, was too insubstantial to take a heavy brooch and other jewels reflected this. Some, like the Milanese-chain bracelets, seemed to mimic the voluptous texture of the new fabric. Many of the gold-mesh purses of the twenties have now gone into the melting pot and considering that they may contain as much as six or eight ounces of 18-carat gold, the wonder is that any have slipped through the clutches of the dealer in 'old gold' at all. The fashion for gold mesh reached its apotheosis in 1926 in a solid gold dress. 'A golden coat of mail is the latest thing in Franco American smart circles in Paris. The precious "shirt of mail" worn by Miss Mabel Bell, a well-known American living in Paris, . . . is the exact replica of the coat worn by knights of the middle ages. It is woven of the finest gold mesh similar to that used in making purses. The blouse is trimmed with platinum. It is necessary to look twice to make sure that it is not silk.'[2]

THE ORIENTAL STYLE

The war only served to whet still further the fashionable appetite for anything oriental. What had been a fad now became a craze which existed at every social and intellectual level. The poignant archetypal figure of T. E. Lawrence and his account of life and violent death in the deserts of Arabia, Valentino's Sheik and Sax Rohmer's Doctor Fu Manchu were all manifestations of our perennial obsession with the East.

The clean lines and earthy colours of Egyptian art were in complete harmony with the spirit of the twenties and the discovery of the tomb of Tut-Ankh-Amen pushed them to the very wavecrest of fashion (Plate 67). The lotus and the papyrus burgeoned everywhere and the jeweller even went so far as to take fragments of the granular blue and green Egyptian faience and blend them cunningly into his work. Cartiers were very successful at this and a belt clasp dating from around 1925 has a rectangular plaque of faience enclosed by a temple portico of sapphires, rubies, diamonds and onyx. It was intended to be worn on a wide band of braided black silk. Indian enamels were given similar treatment (Plate 68).

Another feature of Cartier's work are the cypress-like motifs of Islamic art which the British probably associate more closely with a Paisley print. Fretted out of a

2. *Sphere*, 30 October 1926.

67. (above left) *A calibré-cut sapphire, diamond and carved crystal* BELT CLASP *in a papyrus design. This jewel was advertised by* CARTIER, *the makers, in the* Illustrated London News *of 24 October 1925*

68. (above right) *A* PENDANT *set with a green 'enamel' from Partabgarh, Central India*

69. (below left) *A Cabochon emerald and diamond cypress-tree* BROOCH

70. (below right) *A chinoiserie plaque* BROOCH *in diamond, calibré-cut rubies and navette-shaped emeralds*

straight-sided bracelet or outlined on a brooch with a pencil line of black enamel, other firms copied them, often very successfully (Plate 69).

Chinoiserie designs also occur on jewels (Plate 70) but were usually used to decorate cigarette cases, powder cases and what the collector chooses to call 'objects of virtu'. They weave a rare sortilege in which the workmanship is as precious as the materials, and the subjects, simple as a fairy tale, are contrasted with the extreme sophistication of the technique. Tiny figures hurry through willow-pattern landscapes of islands, pagodas and sampans often depicted in black and sealing-wax red champlevé enamel which cunningly suggest coromandel lacquer. *Bonsai*, the artificially dwarfed trees beloved of the Japanese now began to appear alongside the aspidistras in some British homes. They became popular as a decorative motif too, picked out in rose diamonds or marcasite on the lid of a lacquered or enamelled case.

COLOUR AND THE LAPIDARY

Art deco, whilst reacting against art noveau, inherited from it the imagination to use the whole range of jewellers' skills and even add to the repertoire. Colour was important in the twenties, strong colour, earthy and unrefined: *eau-de-Nil*, ultramarine, *sang-de-boeuf*, raw orange and black, and for this palette, the jeweller looked not only to the lacquer and the enamel worker but also and above all to the lapidary. Jade, closest in colour to the *eau-de-Nil* of fashion came ready carved from China and so did lapis lazuli, blue chalcedony and coral.

Fashion made new demands on the European lapidary too. In Europe the great commercial lapidary centre is Idar Oberstein, West Germany, where, over the centuries, the working of precious minerals has grown into a considerable industry. Here onyx, cornelian and crystal were not only shaped to the conventional forms required by the makers of hat brooches, Creole earrings, link bracelets and the like but stained with the fashionable colours of the day. Agate is slightly porous and will in time absorb a colouring agent so that dull-grey agate can be transmuted into the semblance of glowing cornelian, onyx both black and striped, verdant chrysoprase or lavender jade, and the crudest hornstone transformed into azure 'Swiss lapis'.

Once again coral became fashionable although the demand was now for the deep *sang-de-boeuf* tints, not the pallid 'angel skin' pinks of the previous decade. In the *Sphere* of December 1929 we read 'coral is raging in Paris like some genial form of scarlet fever. It must be as red as possible and even the most solid lumps of it carved in a block or wired together, are sought after—you know the frightful bracelets and brooches that father's great aunt left mother. Yes just those. The pink sort is not in evidence. . . . The dandy way to use the pink red coral of today's fancy is to mix it with the bluest lapis lazuli you can find.' Obviously the Neapolitan confections of the 1860s were being given a new lease of life by the twenties flapper. A fashion plate of 1925 shows a girl wearing a choker necklace and a bracelet of huge coral beads with an enormous coral bouton mounted in her ring. In no sense though does this signal a return to the monumental and crushingly predictable parures of the previous century.

The Twenties

LACQUER

Actually what strikes the eye as enamel in many twenties pieces really is lacquer. Lacquer has some advantages over enamel when it is used in large areas. It is lighter, more pleasant in the hand and gives a better grip. Enamel, although harder than lacquer, is extremely brittle and it is arguable whether it is in fact more durable. Drop a heavy enamel piece and an ugly and almost irreparable chip is practically inescapable—lacquer would probably come out of a similar mishap unscathed.

Lacquering was brought to a high degree of perfection. An absolutely dust-free atmosphere and a very critical balance between temperature and humidity are essential and some of the best lacquers were hardened off in rooms in which a continuous stream of water was kept pouring down the walls. The most refined techniques of the Japanese craftsman were now practised in European workshops, principally in Paris, and almost magical effects were achieved by dusting the hardening lacquer with tiny shards of mother-of-pearl, or embedding crushed eggshells into it. Cigarette and vanity cases were even made in the flattened cylindrical form of an *inro*, the medicament box carried by a Japanese man as part of his traditional dress.

THE GEOMETRIC STYLE

The geometric style of the inter-war years went back in an unbroken line of succession to the jugendstil designs of 1905. After 1918 Futurism and Cubism gave to it an extra impetus. By now the centre of gravity had shifted from Glasgow, Berlin, Vienna and Copenhagen: Paris had become the centre of 'L'Art Decoratif', a supremacy which the exhibition of 1925 affirmed beyond question. Jean Fouquet and Raymond Templier became the high priests of jewel design just as Poiret and Erté were in the world of dress.

Abstraction and stylization gave way to pure geometry and the ultimate triumph of the cylinder, the quadrant and the square. Pleasantly bumpy melon-shaped beads were contrasted with the icy symmetry of diamond-set spheres, discs and cubes in very successful necklaces (Plate 71). Octagons of onyx were studded with a single diamond and mounted in rings, cylinders of onyx and coral, and cones of lapis lazuli were hung from the ears. It was a style as French as the oriental jewels of Cartier and Mauboussin but transplanted less happily into English soil. In London the change of direction was less obvious, but here as in every other fashion centre the geometrical influence grew stronger until by the end of the decade it had crystallized into a style

71. A NECKLACE *of emerald beads, plain and melon-shaped, diamonds and onyx*

which was to persist until after the Second World War. There is little to be said today in favour of these designs of chain links, strapwork, and buckle motifs, with their faintly sinister overtones of sexual bondage, but there is no doubt about it they were very popular for a long time.

Towards the end of the twenties another kind of geometrical decoration began to emerge, apparently quite independently. The origin of these stepped architectural motifs has been looked for in Mayan America as well as in ancient Mesopotamia. Reports in the illustrated magazines of 1928 of the excavation of Ur of the Chaldees with their accounts of treasure trove and lurid hints of human sacrifice would have been more than enough to fuel a popular style. In the previous year, on the other hand, the city of Chumucha was discovered in the jungles of British Honduras. South America seemed to hold out an enormous romantic attraction between the wars. The jungles of Brazil were one of the few remaining unexplored places on earth, concealing head-hunting Indians, snakes as long as goods trains, and, it was said, the golden city of El Dorado in their green labyrinths. Also, the craftwork of the Indians of the American South West had recently been discovered by fashionable New Yorkers. But whether from Babylonian ziggurat, Mayan temple, or Navajo blanket, this hooked, stepped and barbed decoration appeared on all kinds of jewellery in the twenties and thirties.

Lightness and economy were the characteristics of the jewels worn in the early twenties, and only towards the end of the decade were they of massive size or worn in overwhelming quantity. What strikes one most about the jewels worn between 1918 and 1929 is that so many of them originated before the war. Peace did not give the designer the chance to write his own ticket for the decade's fashion. After a war people are too busy trying to get back where they were before the guns went off to make too many changes. Paris had seen something similar a hundred years before when eighteenth-century designs came back after the defeat of Napoleon. It took the economic catastrophe of the late twenties to bring about changes far deeper than any wrought by four years of war.

5 · The Thirties

The year of the Wall Street crash, 1929, brought many changes. A journalist writes with a pomp and circumstance more telling than the logic of his argument: 'Unmourned the period of post war ebullience is passing into oblivion to give place to the newer sanity born of responsibility and grounded in the order and decorum which fundamentally dwell in the heart of every Englishman.'[1] It was not of course the English who determined fashion but the French and the same writer remarks that Frenchmen are no longer interested in women like vicious schoolboys. Hair styles changed, becoming soft, even fluffy, a halo which framed the head rather than a helmet which encased it.

Women became more womanly, meekly returning, it seemed to the gilded cage which history had allotted them. A picture in *Vogue* of 12 December 1934 shows an exquisitely gowned figure loaded with bracelets and photographed against a background of iron bars and, as the caption says: 'The finely wrought iron gate, the heavy bracelets make Mrs Goodenay look like a decorative prisoner in her gown sewn with tiny sequins.'

There was a mood of romanticism abroad, of dressing up, which evoked, often quite self-consciously, the 1830s and 1840s. *The Barretts of Wimpole Street* played to packed houses in Paris and Lucien Bogaert's fragile, languid Elizabeth, exquisitely gowned by Molyneux, was admired and imitated by Parisiennes. By day it was Cromwell collars, Jacobin jackets, muffs, tricornes and cossack hats, by night the 'picture frock', a dream of Renoir, Rubens or Winterhalter which was no longer 'created' by the designer but, according to the fashion journalists, 'expressed'.

To believe that this new trend to romantic femininity would result in jewels that were light and delicate would be to misunderstand it completely. The very opposite was the case. The extreme preciousness of the materials from which jewels are made seldom allows them to blend completely into the general scheme of dress. At the very least they are a foil, a complement, a highlight and at times a dramatic and explosive contrast. The massive bracelets and clips of the thirties were intended by their

1. *Sphere*, 7 November 1931.

crushing weight and lacerating angularity to emphasize the tenderness and vulnerability of the female creature. Few concessions were made to animate nature: some ruthlessly stylized leaves and flowers; some birds which look as though they might have been activated by clockwork. The rest was mainly rings and ribbons, straps and buckles; if a haberdasher had sat down with a harness-maker to evolve a jewellery style one cannot help feeling that this would have been the result (Plate 87).

CLIPS AND DOUBLE CLIPS

If one had to choose a single jewel to represent the whole period there is no doubt that it would have to be the clip. Clips not only came close to displacing the conventional brooch, but they were used in ways which would have been impossible for any other jewel. The typical clip was mitre-shaped and provided with a sprung fastening which clasped the edge of the garment rather than impaled it with a pin (Plate 72). In such a gadget-ridden, novelty-seeking age it was probably inevitable that clips, which were usually worn in pairs anyway, should come to be mounted on a frame as a brooch. These double clips could be of intimidating size—up to four inches in width. The limitations of the design, far from inhibiting the designer, seem to have goaded him to furious efforts of originality. In the simplest and earliest type both clips are symmetrical and identical. There were others in which the clips were identical and

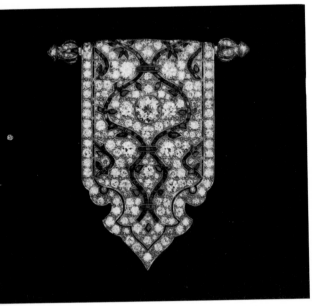

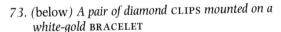

72. (left) A diamond and calibré-cut ruby CLIP

73. (below) A pair of diamond CLIPS *mounted on a white-gold* BRACELET

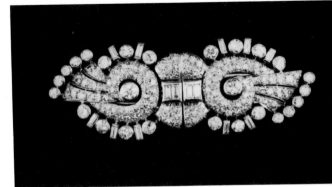

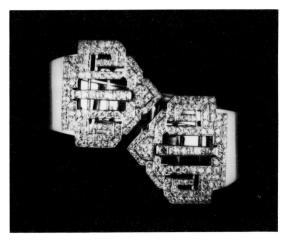

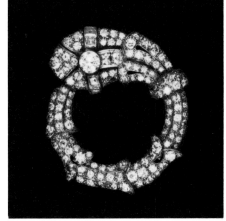

74. *A diamond double-clip* BROOCH *in a volute design of the later thirties*

75. *A diamond circle* CLIP

asymmetrical so that when put together left to army left, as it were, the effect is as though the double-clip brooch had been twisted in the middle (Plate 73). When two asymmetrical clips were made so that one was the mirror image of the other, the brooch was symmetrical about a vertical central axis. The most recent designs started with two asymmetrical motifs, like sprays of flowers, which combined into another asymmetrical form.

In 1936 the conventional dual purpose of the double clip was extended still further by mounting it at the front of a bracelet, a smooth, flat band of gold, platinum or black lacquer (enamel would not be flexible enough for this purpose). Circular, leaf or mitre-shaped clips were usually chosen for this style (Plate 74).

A year later in 1937 small clips were made in sets of four, or even six. These miniature clips could be worn in many ways: all together on the neckline or lapels or singly on the scarf or handbag. Complete sets are unusual, but individual clips in the form of an enamelled and turbanned blackamoor's head, a lapis lazuli and diamond scarab, a diamond rose, or the lacquered head of a Red Indian brave, usually bearing the name of Cartier, are not uncommon.

As originally conceived the clip fastening was a hinged and sprung flap, sometimes with serrated jaws to grip the fabric more securely. In 1937 this was replaced with two curved prongs, an arrangement which was lighter and kinder to the clothing it was worn on.

Another clip, quite unrelated to any of these, was designed as an open circle of gems, broken to admit the hem of the fabric which was then secured with a little spiked latch (Plate 75). Boucheron produced several versions of the circle clip.

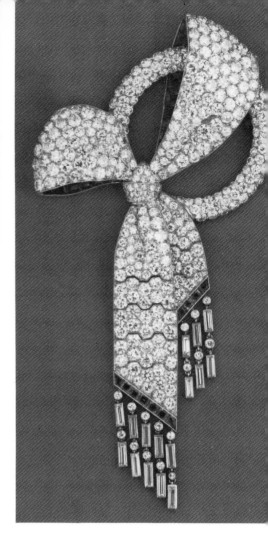

76. (left) *A diamond* BROOCH, *the large stones almost invisibly secured between two circles of black enamel,* c.1930

77. (centre) *A diamond and pearl* BROOCH, c.1930, *possibly from* MAPPIN AND WEBB

78. (right) *A diamond* BROOCH, *the ribbon bow lined with calibré-cut emeralds, actual size,* c.1930

BROOCHES AND PINS

Circular brooches were just as popular and several designs were current around 1930 (Plates 76, 77). The most spectacular variation was a big plain ring tied at one side with a bow of wide ribbon with immensely long trailing ends. The whole was closely pavé with circular-cut diamonds and fringed with baguettes (Plate 78).

In 1934 the 'super safety-pin' was reckoned by *Vogue* to be 'the smartest way of fastening your belt, flowers or scarf'.[2] Safety-pins were worn throughout the thirties and were of gold and carved coral or lapis lazuli (Plate 79). The sort of male who haunted the pages of the glossies was photographed wearing a similar trinket in his neckerchief, only his was in saddle-stitched pigskin.[3]

2. *Vogue*, May 1934.
3. *Sphere*, September 1928.

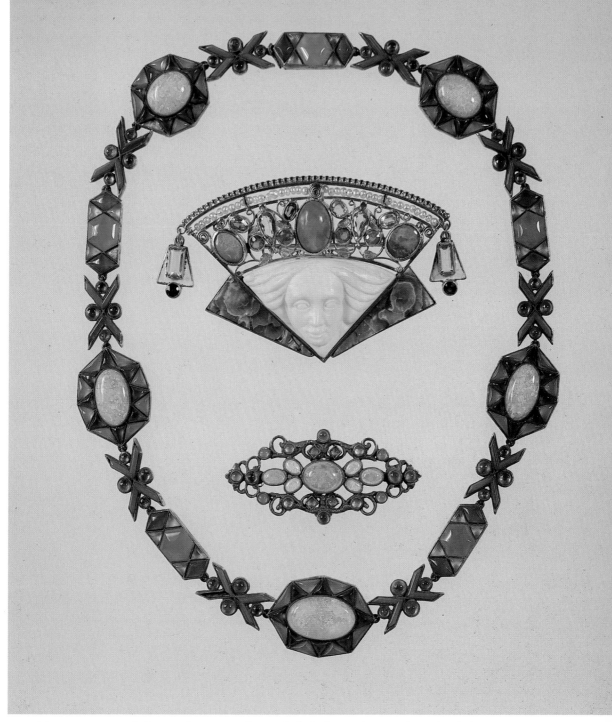

XII. *(a) A* NECKLACE *of silver, opal, garnet and stained chalcedony in 'carpet of gems' style by*
SYBIL DUNLOP. See page 85
(b) A carved ivory, mother-of-pearl, opal, tourmaline, pearl and crystal BROOCH *by* GEORGE
HUNT.
(c) A silver, opal, garnet and stained chalcedony BROOCH *by* SYBIL DUNLOP. See page 85
Courtesy of the Victoria and Albert Museum

XIII. 'Crown of Thorns', a NECKLACE *of gold, coral, onyx, mother-of-pearl and fossil ammonites
by* SAH OVED. *See page 86*

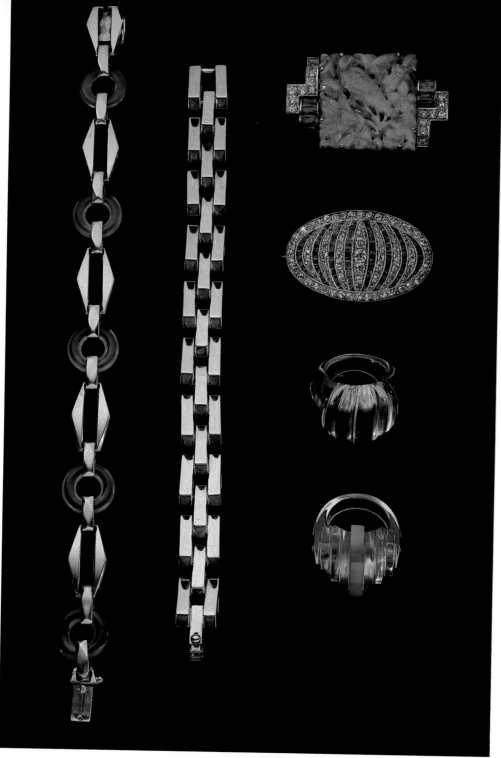

XIV. (a) A gold and cornelian BRACELET. See page 80
(b) A gold and lapis lazuli 'moving staircase' BRACELET. See page 101
(c) A Chinese carved-jade, ruby and diamond BROOCH in zigzag design. See page 103
(d) A diamond and calibré-cut sapphire BROOCH.
(e) A carved crystal RING. See page 103
(f) A crystal and stained chalcedony RING. See page 103

XV. *(a) An aquamarine and diamond* BRACELET. See page 107
   (b) A ruby and diamond BRACELET. See page 101
   (c) A citrine and gold BRACELET. *See page 107*

XVI. (a) *An aquamarine and diamond* CLIP *by* CARTIER. *See page* 107
  (b) *An aquamarine and diamond* BROOCH *of the late thirties; the setting of the briolette drop is later. See page* 107
  (c) *A pair of citrine and diamond rosette-shaped* EARCLIPS. *See page* 107
  (d) *A citrine and diamond flower* CLIP *by* CARTIER. *See page* 107

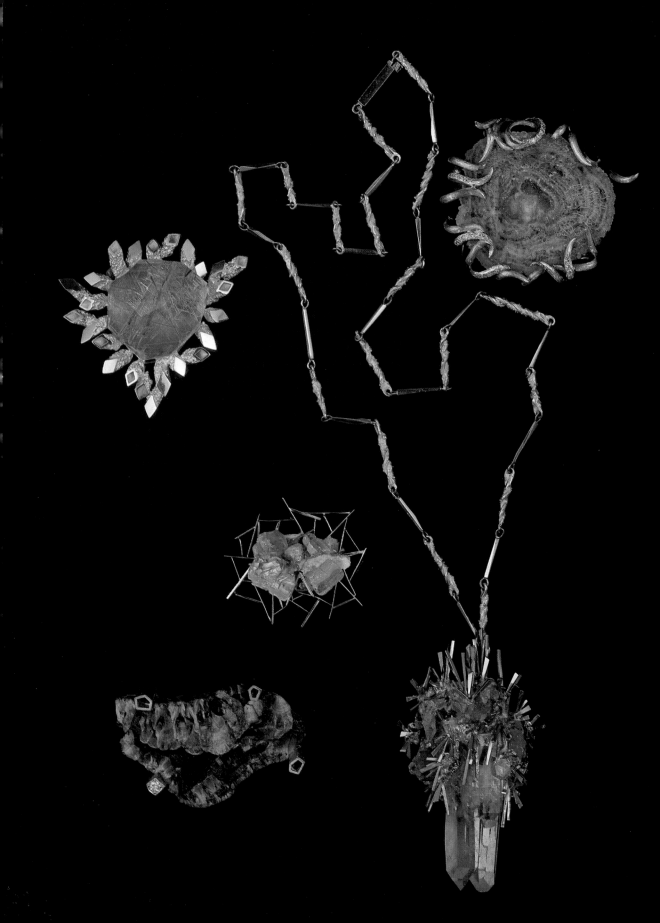

XVIII. *A* COLLAR *of gold, diamonds and enamel, by* THELMA ROBERTSON, *winner of de Beers 1969 Diamonds International Award (reduced).* See page 143

XIX. *A titanium and diamond* RING *by* JOEL DEGEN, *awarded first prize in the engagement ring category of de Beers' Diamonds Today Competition, 1981 (enlarged).* See page 158

XVII. (*opposite*) *(a) An 18-carat gold and diamond* BROOCH *set with a desert-rose agate, by* ANDREW GRIMA. See page 142
  (b) An 18-carat gold and pink Venus-hair stone BROOCH *by* JOHN DONALD. See page 124
  (c) An 18-carat gold and wulfenite BROOCH *by* JOHN DONALD. See page 124
  (d) An 18-carat white and yellow gold PENDANT *set with quartz crystals, by* DAVID THOMAS. See page 121
  (e) An 18-carat gold, diamond and uncut malachite BROOCH *by* ANDREW GRIMA. See page 142
  Courtesy of the Worshipful Company of Goldsmiths

XX. *(a) Niobium* BRACELET *by* CLARISSA MITCHELL. See page 149
      (b) Niobium EARRINGS *by* CLARISSA MITCHELL. See page 149

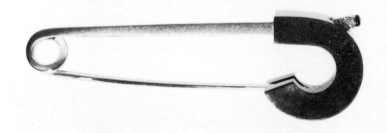

79. *A gold, lapis lazuli, rose-diamond and enamel safety-pin* BROOCH

The most popular brooch of all was a more or less rectangular plaque in a design of heavy open strapwork pavé-set with diamonds. Thousands of them are in existence and thousands more must have perished at the hands of the breaker. Plaque brooches were the vehicle for every design motif and gimmick of the period, drape and ribbon, link and buckle, Mexican steps, chinoiseries and stylized flowers (Plates 80, 81, 82). The diamonds with which they were set were of every cut and quality, the mounts of platinum or white gold. Coloured stones in this type of jewel were less usual.

80. (right) *A diamond plaque* BROOCH *of strap and buckle motifs*

81. (below left) *A small diamond plaque* BROOCH *pierced in a stepped design. Strong diagonals are characteristic of the early thirties*

82. (below right) *A diamond* BROOCH *in a bombé openwork design. This pattern was advertised by the Goldsmiths' and Silversmiths' Company in 1929*

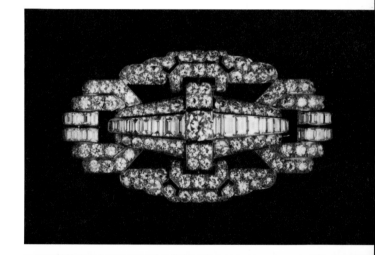

The Thirties

ANTIQUES

As with the clothes they wore, women looked back to early Victorian times for their jewellery. Antique jewels were once again in demand and women all too often committed the unspeakable vulgarity of having the pleasantly tarnishable settings of old diamond jewels smothered with tinselly rhodium plate or even 'washed' with gold. Most efforts actually to reproduce old jewellery, like the disembodied hand brooches of 1840 or the tasselled designs of twenty years later, were confined to costume jewellery. The strap and buckle bracelets popularized by Van Cleef and Arpels are an exception since they do have an affinity with the Victorian jarretière. The design was a broad strap of honeycomb or brick-pattern linking often richly buckled with gems and it was deservedly popular for some years (Plate 83). A cheap version of this type of linking in chromium plate was used for bracelets and purses, marketed under the name of 'radior'.

83. A gold, diamond and cabochon ruby jarretière BRACELET

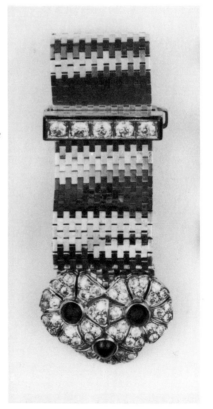

84. *A diamond and chalcedony bead* BRACELET

BRACELETS

Bracelets were still worn several at a time and next to the clip were the most popular jewel of the thirties. A very successful design was of four or more rows of pearls or beads with two or three diamond ornaments at intervals. The beads might be of precious stones — rubies, sapphires or emeralds — or of mere ornamental hardstones like crocidolite, onyx or stained-green chalcedony (Plate 84). Pearl necklaces were strung in a similar way, in several rows with a diamond motif at either side of the

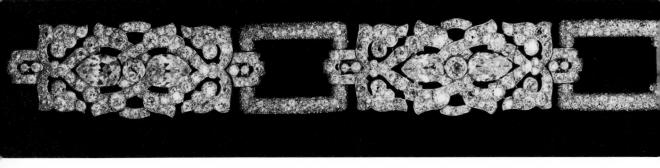

85. A diamond BRACELET *in a design of oriental lilies and bombé links, c. 1929*

86. A cabochon sapphire and diamond BRACELET*, c. 1930*

87. A diamond BRACELET *of chain-link and buckle design*

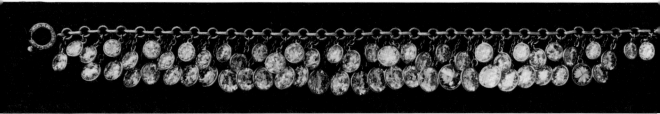

88. A diamond BRACELET *probably inspired by an Indian dancing-girl's anklet (*slightly
reduced*)*

festooned front and a big clasp at the back. This design idea was echoed in bracelets set with more conventionally cut gems (Colour Plate XVb).

Designs were massive—'chunky' as the fashion journalist would say—better to have one big bracelet than several small ones. At their most forbidding these diamond bracelets could be heavier than anything worn by the Victorians; big pavé-set plaques joined in threes or vast squared chain-links which seem in their inhibiting weight and manacle-like appearance more fitted to some half-forgotten race at the fringe of civilization than the smart set of London, New York and Paris (Plates 85, 86, 87).

It was important that bracelets should be heard as well as seen with links and pendants that clanked and jingled with every movement (Plate 88). In 1938 Asprey's were even selling gilded cowbell jewels at fifty-four shillings for a bracelet and thirty-seven and sixpence for earclips.

The jeweller has never been averse to using a little optical trick to get an effect. The moving staircase bracelet of 1934 employs just such a *trompe-l'œil* effect—checkered steps gem-set and polished so that from one angle the eye meets bland polished metal and from the opposing direction a dazzle of coloured stones (Colour Plate XIVb).

Makers of fashion jewellery were not slow to take up such a fetching gimmick and the shops were soon offering cheap versions in chromium and paste. The wooden bracelets of 1930 were another inexpensive novelty; prisms of inlaid hardwood threaded on thin elastic, like the Victorian expanding bracelet.

EARRINGS

Throughout the decade hair was either cut short or piled high upon the head. Seldom did it cover the ears, so that earrings were just as popular as they had been in the years just after the war. In 1934 neat nautilus or scallop shells, stylized wing motifs or leaves set with diamonds were in fashion (Plate 89). For dress occasions long diamond drops, or droopy girandoles 'à la Pompadour' were the thing (Plate 90), and for the unheirloomed majority manufacturers produced convincing imitations in paste and silver. Earrings did not escape the craze for convertibility and they were sometimes made to combine with a brooch to make an even bigger brooch.

1939 was, if *Vogue* magazine is to be believed, 'a year for ears',[4] and fashion columnists proffered earnest advice about how to make the most of them—a blush of rouge on the lobe if they were too long, or on the tip to provide a rosy background to a single pearl. For no longer were earrings of necessity clamped to the lobe of the ear.

4. *Vogue*, 8 February 1939.

The Thirties

Many new designs curved upwards following its outline, formed as leaves or flowers, or a breaking wave (Plate 91), sometimes with a diamond drop trembling beneath it. With the hair scraped up and away on top of the head the naked ears seemed to be crying out for garnish and adornment and a huge range of ornaments was devised from dainty drops to huge cluster clips.

Hair styles became more elaborate and in 1935 the tiara made a come-back, eventually replacing the simpler bandeau. 'Pile it on,' urged *Vogue*, 'the fantasy, the fun. Top your distinguished head with all manner of flora and feathers, tweaks and twists of velvet and lamé.'[5]

THE PARISIANS

It was as ever the Parisian jewellers whose influence was strongest and most of the important ones had a retail shop in London: Chaumet, Mauboussin, Boucheron, and of course Cartier. Cartier were as important as ever, but after 1929 the firm of Mauboussin became known for jewels which captured unerringly the paradoxical spirit of *chic*: zigzag designs which flicker from side to side like summer lightning. The tube ring was their invention, a short cylinder of platinum and diamonds into which the finger slipped naturally and comfortably, the front pavé with diamonds, orthodox brilliants and baguettes and the whole gamut of 'fancy-cuts': triangle, trapeze, keystone, obus and lunette. The back was fretted out to a mere skeleton outline.

But it was probably Herz, another Parisian firm, which from 1934 had the biggest

5. *Vogue*, 19 February 1935.

89. (above) *A pair of pearl and diamond* EARCLIPS

90. (right) *A pair of emerald and diamond pendent* EARRINGS

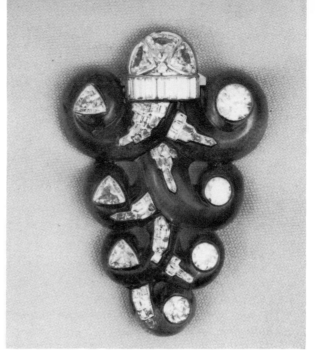

91. (below) *A pair of ruby and diamond* EARCLIPS

92. (right) *A carved smoky-quartz and diamond* CLIP *by* HERZ *of Paris*

influence on jewel fashions on both sides of the Channel. Herz carried the trend towards massive simplicity to its logical conclusion and these jewels have a look of monumental simplicity as though they have been hewn from the living rock. In a sense many of them were: carved *en bloc* from smoke-grey chalcedony or dark molasses quartz (Plate 92). Bracelets are among the most successful of the Herz jewels. Often they are without hinge or catch: a simple opening at the back is just wide enough to allow the bracelet to be squeezed on to the wrist oriental style. Huge as they are, these shapely ingots of gold and blocks of chalcedony with citrines or diamonds plugged into their gleaming surfaces as though with a riveting-gun are yet so right that to call them clumsy would not merely be inaccurate but also quite irrelevant.

Interest in carved hardstone seems to have quickened in the mid-thirties (Colour Plate XIVe and f). Garrards offered brooches in onyx and crystal striped with horizontal bands of diamonds, and crystal clips studded with rubies. Onyx was always lapped to a brilliant polish and rock crystal usually given a frosted translucent finish. Costume jewellers were not slow to follow suit and countless imitations were made in moulded glass.

CHINESE AND INDIAN DESIGNS

The orientalism of the twenties which had lost some of its momentum in the early thirties was quickened by the Chinese Exhibition of 1935 (Colour Plate XIVc). The

93 (a and b). A
   collapsible gold and
   tortoiseshell
   CIGARETTE
   HOLDER

fashion colours of 1936 were Peking yellow, lotus-bud pink, Manchu brown and celadon green. Jade was back and so were chinoiseries of every description. Even in her make-up the fashionable woman affected an almond-eyed Far-Eastern look. Crystal plaques were carved with intaglio dragons and set in pendants. For £7 15s Tiffany's of Bond Street would sell you a black and scarlet lacquer cigarette case—'a charming piece of English chinoiserie' according to the 1935 Christmas edition of *Vogue*.

Indian jewels were very popular too, especially just before the war. Schiaparelli even copied the tasselled fastenings of Indian necklaces, and the fringes and pendants which enlivened so many jewels undoubtedly came from the same source. Bib necklaces which had a deep fringe of pendants at the front are obviously of Eastern origin and the resemblance between the fringed bracelets of the thirties and the wrist and ankle ornaments of a nautch girl are too close to be coincidental (Plate 88).

SMOKING

Between the First World War and the lung cancer scares of the fifties smoking had not yet acquired its modern stigma and was still a perfectly respectable social habit.

In fact it was a good deal more than this: one has only to recall the sleight-of-hand with which Fred Astaire taps a cigarette on its slim case or the boyish cameraderie with which Clark Gable ignites two at once to sense that here was a secular ritual as significant in its way as the Japanese tea ceremony. Smoking had its own superstitions and taboos and its own peculiar impedimenta. In 1930 a competition was held to celebrate the four hundredth anniversary of the introduction of tobacco. There were two prizes: one for the man who could keep his pipe alight the longest; the other for the lady who could most elegantly smoke a cigarette. The lady winner, a Mlle Claude Loti, was photographed clasping what appears to be a stuffed leopard in her arms as she drags seductively at a *caporal*.

The jeweller did his best to satisfy a craving for more and newer gadgets which was almost as ferocious as the desire for the weed itself. Cigarette holders were invented to cool the smoke and protect the fingers from nicotine stains: some were a foot and a half long, the clichéd stage prop of the twenties flapper; others were telescopic and packed into a tiny case smaller than a thimble and some took apart like a fishing rod (Plate 93). Ejector holders jettisoned the glowing fag-end without the indignity of burned fingers. Less common are those that gripped the cigarette in a little pair of gold tongs projecting from a finger ring, freeing the hand (Plate 94). Amber was the

94. An unusual gold CIGARETTE HOLDER

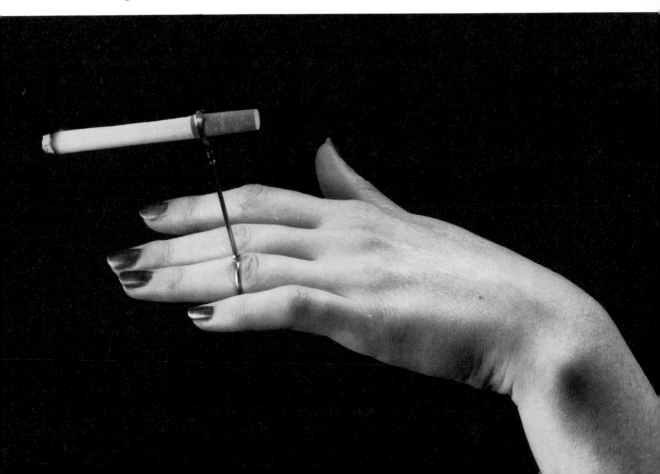

95. *A gold* CIGARETTE CASE
*incorporating lighter, watch,
lipstick, pencil and mirror,
sometimes called a minaudière*

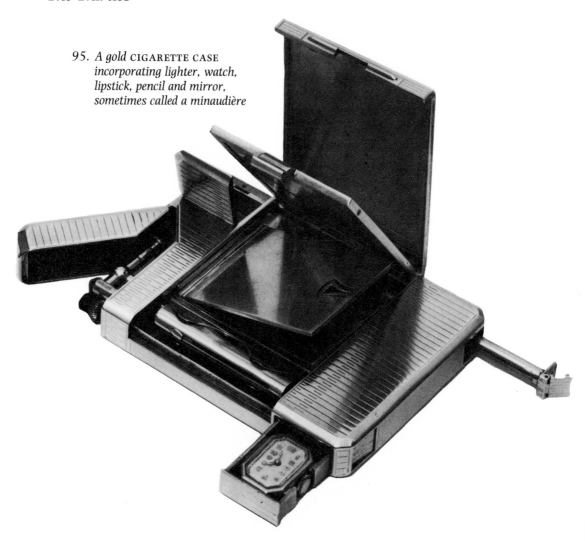

traditional material, originally used for a similar purpose in the Middle East because of an age-old belief that it would not transmit infection, but there were also cigarette holders of ivory, crystal, onyx and jade.

The case-maker brought a similar ingenuity to his craft (Plate 95). Some cases combined the functions of watch and lighter, others had a secret catch so that only the initiated could open them. Asprey's made one with a sliding hinge that opened in response to a deft conjuror's gesture.

COLOUR IN JEWELS

After 1925 dress fashions tended towards the dark and dramatic with the emphasis on cut rather than colour. It was the age of the 'little black dress' brilliantly highlighted with jewels. 'Under your coat—it's black again—and with your simple dress jewels become terribly important. Sometimes they will even influence the choice of dress. We watched one woman turn down a Molyneux black wool dress for another with a far less exciting neckline because she possesses two magnificent Herz diamond and crystal clips that wanted no interference.'[6]

Towards the end of the thirties there was a change in jewel fashions led by Herz and Cartier as the emphasis shifted from diamonds to coloured stones and to certain semi-precious stones in particular. In 1937 it was aquamarines and diamonds (Colour Plates XVa, XVIa and b), the aquamarines often step-cut and set in platinum together with diamond brilliants and baguettes. The designs were unremarkable—conventional geometrical motifs joined by flat pavé-set chains, but the cool mix of summer blue aquamarine with the frosty fire of diamonds is a happy one.

As colour became more important to the jeweller, gold in contrasting hues of red, yellow and white (green was seldom used at this time) began in some measure to take the place of platinum. This was a natural consequence of the popularity of coloured stones as the warmer-toned gems only look their best in a gold setting (Plate 96).

The monetary value of a stone became less important, colour was what really mattered, and for a while the diamond was edged into second place by aquamarines, topazes, rubies and amethysts. There can be no doubt though that it was jewels set with the yellow and brown stones, golden sapphires, canary and cinnamon diamonds and above all topazes and citrines which were the *succès fou* of the last two years of peace (Colour Plate XVc).

In 1938 Cartier launched a range of citrine jewels which were perhaps the finest of the inter-war period. The designs were simple, upsetting none of the conventions of the day: their piquancy lay in the gold settings and in the colour of the stones which were often selected in two contrasting shades, honey yellow and Vandyke brown. Flower designs were most popular (Colour Plate XVIc and d), especially the famous 'Cartier Daisy'. Topazes and citrines were in great demand and antique jewels set with the tawny gems were hunted out in a holocaust of melting down and resetting.

Not all of the innovations between the wars were so beneficial to the jeweller: one new development brought hardship to many and to some bankruptcy. For years the Japanese had been researching a method of farming pearls, seeding the oyster with a

6. *Vogue*, 2 October 1935.

shell-bead nucleus and then husbanding and harvesting it under controlled conditions. Patents were granted in 1914 and in 1921 the full implications of the cultured pearl burst upon the London market. Millions of pounds were wiped off the value of stock overnight. All trading in pearls ceased until a positive means could be devised of detecting in a pearl the presence of the tell-tale nucleus. The answer was the endoscope, an instrument resembling a minute periscope which could be introduced into the drill hole of a pearl so as to illuminate it from the inside. In time the gemmologist evolved a battery of techniques and instruments, but in spite of this the pearl trade continued to languish. It has never recovered and pearls, particularly on the London market, have never altogether won back the admiration they once excited.

6 · The Second World War and After— 1939–1960

The 1939 conflict was a propaganda war with all the resources of the media harnessed to the task of keeping the nation cheerful, stoical and aggressive. Naturally this had its effect on fashion. Widows' weeds were out—not only did they weaken morale, but they were very difficult to see in the blackout. Colours had to be bright and look well with khaki or blue.

Tens of thousands of women were in uniform and to them all but the barest minimum of jewellery was forbidden. The khaki ATS were allowed cufflinks—*Vogue* recommended the H-shaped variety which were easy to insert. Leather was felt to have a sporty practicality which went best with khaki, but for the better-heeled topaz or citrine had the advantage of looking good and of being right in the latest pre-war fashion. Without a handbag powder compacts became a problem so the flapjack was devised—slim and circular it could be slipped into a uniform pocket without raising a non-regulation bulge.

The supply of platinum was controlled 'for the duration' and details of stocks had to be declared to the government—not so much because of a shortage as to prevent its being smuggled to the enemy.[1] The real shortage was of manpower. Besides the many who joined the armed forces, countless fine craftsmen were sucked into munitions work and the men in Cartier's workshops found themselves making camera parts and navigational instruments.

The ghost of pre-war fashion still glimmered here and there in the few jewels which struggled through the all-enveloping meshes of the war effort. Fishy subaqueous motifs, starfish, nautilus and leaping fish served to remind us, together with whale-meat steaks and Ministry of Food fishcakes, that Britain still ruled the waves. 'Noisy' jewels—chain bracelets from which coins, medallions or antique watch-seals clashed and jangled had been very popular just before the war. With the blackout anything which announced a pedestrian's approach was a godsend. Hindu dancers'

1. Order of the War Production Board dated 30 May 1942.

toe-bells depending from a lapel clip, bangles worn a dozen at a time, charm bracelets or chains fringed with gilt almonds or walnuts undoubtedly owed some of their popularity to this. Luminous costume jewellery—plastic Scottie dog brooches, for example—was also made for wear in the blackout. Smarter jewellers produced 'Tom Thumb' flashlights no bigger than a lipstick in engine-turned silver.

In the front line of course visibility could mean death from a sniper's bullet. Fortnum's sold a cigarette lighter which worked on the tinder-box principle and glowed rather than burned brightly. Cigarette cases were engraved with the menacing outline of an ack-ack gun and little silver spitfires formed charms and brooches. Identity discs, now worn by the civil as well as military population, hid their grim function behind other shapes, hearts, or the friendly rotundities of a barrage balloon. Cheerfully coloured plastic hair-slides and clips were bought in their thousands by munitions workers for keeping their hair under the enveloping head scarf and out of the machines. Badge brooches and cufflinks enamelled with regimental colours were naturally very popular. Patriotic jewellery was much less in evidence than it had been in 1914, although Spitfires, victory Vs and torches of liberty were quite plentiful, and crosses of Lorraine for those with Free French boyfriends. German and Italian POWs here in Britain whiled away the years of captivity making rings out of perspex 'aeroplane glass' just as in occupied Norway Russian prisoners made rings out of spoons in return for an apple or a piece of bread.

Obviously the war years saw little advance in either design or technique, and ideas, such as they were, were drawn from the staider elements of thirties design. The jewels of *Dorrie Nossiter* had more in common with an earlier Arts and Crafts tradition than with any new emergent style. Her designs rely almost entirely upon the colours of the gems with which they are set for their effect, chromatic harmonies and contrasts rather than shapes and textures (Plate 96). The stones sit in light claw-settings—topazes, pearls, haematites, peridots and amethysts clustered in cheerful agglomerations—earrings that curl right around the ear with pearl drops trembling below, or fan-shaped clips for wearing on the cuff of a short sleeve.

In October 1944 Paris was liberated and Molyneux, Schiaparelli, Boucheron and Cartier could once again assert their benign tyranny over London fashions. It was a long way from business as usual, however. At Gervais the only hair-dryers in Paris were operated by relays of tandem cyclists with a resourcefulness and tenacity which, had it been deployed on the Maginot line, might have changed the course of history.

Victory in 1945 was a shock from which we have never truly recovered. Peace-time continued an austerity unrelieved by the excitement of battle and the hope of a shining new world. The lights had gone up in London—on demob suits, spivs, rationing and the five-bob restaurant limit. Purchase tax, introduced in 1940

96. *A silver* SÛRETÉ PIN *set with coloured stones and baroque pearls,* by DORRIE NOSSITER

97. *A coloured gold and emerald* fir-cone BROOCH

continued to be levied on jewellery at a penal rate, and yet in spite of this the jeweller did very nicely. Up and down the country stowed in carrier bags and biscuit tins under stairs and floorboards was a king's ransom in grubby bank notes which had never seen the light of a tax return—the illicit fruits of black-market cash deals during six years of war. Rumours that the old currency was to be called in and exchanged for bank notes of a different colour caused panic buying of the most concealable, portable, alternative currency to be had—jewellery. A roaring trade sprang up in tax-free second-hand jewels of all kinds, most of them made before the war. Prices rocketed but since the buyers were more interested in the stones than in their settings it was not a trend that did much to stimulate exciting and creative design.

Economic circumstances and the worst kind of stick-in-the-mud British conservatism together helped to keep designs very close to where they were in 1935. Fresh influences from France or the United States (Plate 97) were rapidly dulled and subverted to the prevailing mechanistic awfulness and this was to go on, one step forward and one step back until the late fifties. 'Chunkiness' remained the be-all and end-all of design and nothing embodied this rather dubious quality more completely than cocktail jewellery. Like so many other fashions of the time cocktail rings originated before the war. They tended to be large, and compounded mainly of scroll,

98. Cocktail RINGS *of the forties*

cylinder, prism and trapeze motifs but they were interesting in that they were often not only geometrical but asymmetrical (Plate 98). Cocktail watches were of similar design (Plate 99), the dial often covered by a little hinged lid, the sides either of looped Brazilian chain or that spiralled tubular linking that the trade calls 'gaspipe'. This chain was used for necklaces and bracelets too. But the most persistently popular bracelet was a wide gold band of basket linking, the individual links deeply grooved and fluted, which was worn continually well into the fifties.

Lapel brooches now began to replace the clip—bunches of mechanical looking flowers clustered with rubies and diamonds, the leaves and petals in flashing red and yellow gold, not so much jewellery as sheet-metal work. This was a favoured combination for jewels of every description, the rubies often synthetic because supplies of the natural stones from the mines in Burma and Siam had been interrupted by the war in the Far East (Plate 100).

Jewels inspired by the antique were as popular as they had been just before the war. In 1948 Cartier was selling cigarette cases in the Fabergé manner, deeply

99. A gold, ruby and diamond cocktail WATCH

112

grooved and reeded in a sunray pattern and complete to the cabochon sapphire thumbpiece. In the same year Fortnum's offered pinchbeck vanity cases that counterfeited an antique watch, and in 1949 Ciro's would sell you a creditable imitation of a Victorian diamond star brooch in paste. Silver snuff boxes of the 1830s were lovingly reproduced to contain cigarettes, for it was still smart to smoke. Cigarette cases of the new miracle plastic perspex were ingeniously designed to break and offer two cigarettes. Ejector cigarette holders were finished with a saucy tassel or a little bird perched on the end.

Jewels which won prizes in exhibitions and places in competitions, far from giving a lead to the trade, seemed to lag behind it by at least a decade although this could have been as much the fault of the judges as the designers. A chestnut-spray clip at the Britain Can Make It Exhibition of 1946 could, apart from a certain lightness and

100. *A gold and calibré-cut ruby and diamond* BRACELET *(slightly reduced)*

incisiveness, have been made in 1938. Illustrations in an article on 'Training Craftsmen for Industry'[2] show a round openwork brooch of angel fish streaming through a submarine landscape by *Joan Baker*, and floral brooches in silver and combined metals by *Joyce Jones* and *Barbara Hills* recall the Vienna Sezession with overtones of Disney. Second prize in a competition run by the design research centre of the gold, silver and jewellery industries was won by *H. G. Mautner* with a brooch, ring and earrings. The brooch was a traditional bouquet sketched out in scrolled platinum wire, the ring constructed in light cagework. Economy of design and materials struck the correct note of utility and austerity, but it was the use of light wire that pointed out the direction in which design was to move in the future.

Before the war the jeweller tended to block in his designs with solid gold and platinum and massed pavé-set gems, now he began to pencil them in with an outline of wire either plain or twisted. It was a leitmotif which could be sensed throughout all

2. *Art and Industry*, July 1948.

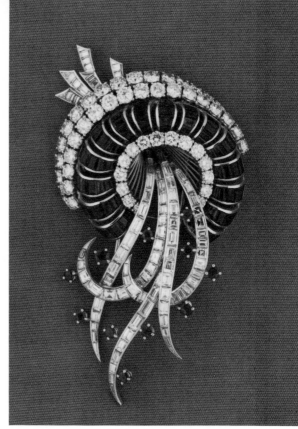

101. (above) *An emerald and diamond* BROOCH

102. (right) *A diamond and emerald flower fantasy*
BROOCH

the visual arts from the brilliant scribblings of Felix Topolsky to the cobweb fantasies
of the Festival of Britain. Now in the botanical designs which had become so popular
for lapel brooches, leaf and petal had been reduced to a fragile autumnal skeleton
lightly touched in with corded wire (Plate 101). The so-called acorn clip had a cluster
of these openwork leaves, each with a central rib of circular-cut diamonds springing
from a peculiarly phallic flowerhead. The resemblance to an acorn was fairly casual,
and the impression was of something exotic and equatorial.

'Flower fantasies' of one kind and another proliferated, amazing orchidaceous
growths, real man-eaters with tormented petals and evil swaying stamens (Plate 102).
In the post-war Britain of savage winters, strikes and fuel shortages it is not difficult to
explain this fashionable preoccupation with the tropics. No justification is needed for
Elizabeth Arden's necklace and bracelet of monkey nuts lacquered in patriotic red,
white and blue—although the British government's ill-fated ground-nut scheme was
very much in the news at the time. There were bracelets of gilt coffee beans and
necklaces of glass oranges, lemons and bananas.

It was in the fifties that we were first able to savour the delights of the package tour.
The British flocked sunwards to the beaches of Spain and Italy and they dressed for
the occasion: Creole earrings big as piston rings in bamboo or colourful plastic,

114

Indian bangles by the jangling dozen set off by complexions bronzed and slick with Ambre Solaire.

Pre-war styles prevailed for a long while alongside the new movement towards lightness and fantasy and for several years after the war the big London shops were advertising diamond jewellery that could have been made in 1930 or even before. After war there is always a great urge to turn the clock back, a yearning for things as they were, and this in itself tends to damp down innovation and postpone change. But change did come and design which had been static and interlocked became more mobile, open and expansive.

The late forties and fifties were a time of transition, slow but certain. Even in 1947 there were signs that fashion was beginning to chafe at the dreary constraints of all those diamond chains, buckles and straps. It was noticeable that the very smartest designs were round rather than square. The smartest dress rings had a domed bezel scattered with tiny gemmed stars or gently swelling bombé shoulders in light scrolled openwork.

Once again in the 1950s movement became important in jewels. Neat earstuds now bore a shimmering cascade of baguettes (Plate 103) or a fernleaf of pendeloques (Plate 104), often detachable so that the tops could be used on less formal occasions. The mobiles which were so popular in the home now appeared as earrings—an Italian idea like so many others at the time. The bib necklace returned with its deep fringe of swaying pendants.

Increasingly designs became loose and casual: 'chunky' gold bracelets were

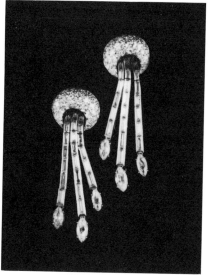

103. (above) *A pair of diamond pendent* EARCLIPS

104. (right) *A pair of diamond* EARCLIPS *with detachable pendants*

105. A diamond BROOCH *of the late fifties*

replaced by a loose plait of tubular chain or a ribbon of gold mesh pinched and gathered at the front by a diamond tie. Even the character of a simple cluster was altered, the supporting gallery replaced by a light cage of platinum wire, the border of petal-like navettes instead of the usual round brilliants. The effect was that of a flower and in the late fifties natural designs like this began to replace the abstraction and rigid stylization of the previous forty years (Plate 105).

7 · The Sixties

By the end of the fifties, the British found themselves at the centre of an empire upon which, contrary to national folklore, the sun was decidedly setting. The process of readjustment to our new place in the world was greatly eased by changes in our personal circumstances. In this topsy-turvy world in which we had won a war only to lose an empire it seemed that as our national status declined the personal wealth of most of us was increasing beyond the wildest dreams of 1939. The average Britisher could now have a car, a washing machine and a holiday in Majorca. The 'affluent society' was upon us and we had 'never had it so good'.

Progress, as it always does, gave with one hand while it took away with the other. Even as we savoured our new wealth and mobility it was dawning upon us that our lives were being diminished in deeply insidious ways. The snug and grubby backstreets were disappearing, replaced by hygienic tower blocks. Plate glass and shuttered concrete replaced blistered paint and soot-patinated brick. At its all-to-frequent worst the new architecture repelled the gaze as effectively as it did the British climate, leaving the eye nothing to linger and pasture on. It was this above all, this fundamental change in the texture of our surroundings which was to exert the deepest influence on the jewel designs of the next decade and to cause a dramatic tilt of the balance away from form and towards texture.

Only a few pockets of the world remained unexplored—the Brazilians were even building a city in the heart of the Matto Grosso. Only the planets remained, and the floor of the world's oceans. New equipment, much of it developed during the war, enabled men to move with freedom beneath the sea, and television allowed us to share its perils and delights with them. This submarine influence is very apparent in jewel designs at this time.

For a nation at peace a lot of shooting was going on and it seemed that no sooner had one 'bush fire' been put out than another sprang up somewhere else. One world war was behind us, but the fear of the next seemed more paralysing than the actual horrors of the blitz. Aldermaston, Bertrand Russell, CND and the four-minute warning were ever in the news and the terror of nuclear war permeated our daily lives. Obsessed with our fears we turned again and again to contemplate the happening we dreaded most in films like *On the Beach* and *The Bed Sitter*. There is an explosive quality in many jewels of the day and a sense of fusion and fission as though they themselves had passed through the nuclear furnace.

Fear of the cataclysm had a secondary effect which was probably more important than the first: it made the 'New Elizabethans' increasingly anxious to spend and enjoy their recently acquired wealth before the big one went off. 'After all,' as everyone was saying at the time, 'you can't take it with you.' Inflation, although not yet in double figures, was still a problem in 1960, enough to encourage people to spend their money as soon as they earned it, sometimes even before.

Patronage and surplus wealth are vital to the jeweller and the sixties provided an abundance of both. As the old icons and sacred cows tumbled we looked for new gods to worship. Adam Faith, first of the new *jeunesse doré*, yodelled his famous question, 'What-do-you-want-if-you-don't-want-mernee?' and his ecstatic teenage audiences bayed back their ravenous answer. As the old class system heaved and cracked around us a new aristocracy was emerging with its own increasingly rigid hierarchy from junior advertising executives to pop stars and film directors. For the jeweller it was to provide a rich source of patronage.

Although wealth was increasing there was a growing unease about displaying it too openly. Crime was on the increase, so was taxation and no one wished to attract the attentions of either the burglar or the tax inspector. Grand state occasions were becoming fewer and further between so the tiara and the parure were on their way out. Two classes of jewellery were emerging: there were jewels 'to put away', usually big stones in the simplest of settings, and jewels for fun. No longer was a fashionable woman expected to carry the weight of the Empire, the white man's burden represented by several hundred carats of diamonds upon her head and shoulders. The only convention was that she should reject convention; she could be herself so she began looking for jewels which would say something about her personality.

At the end of the fifties everything was set for a renaissance in jewellery design. Society was changing and people were assuming new roles in it. As individuals each of us was seeking a new identity and jewellery, the most personal and intimate of the arts, is about identity.

A growing number of young designers, many of them students in other fields, now became attracted by jewellery and looked for someone to teach them this exacting craft. Amazingly, when we consider the progress made in the early years of the century, the art schools let them down and few could now offer courses for the design and making of jewels.

Luckily the Worshipful Company of Goldsmiths and its exhibition secretary Graham Hughes were there with the support, both moral and financial, that was needed. The Goldsmiths were one of the few remaining livery companies to retain their ancient practical function and they were and indeed still are, very actively concerned with the training and examining of apprentices and the hallmarking of precious metals. The Hall is an important patron of the precious crafts but before the war most of its support had gone to the silversmith rather than the jeweller.

Hughes had been virtually brought up with the Goldsmiths as his father was a former clerk of the Company. He himself joined them in 1951 and soon recognized the importance of the new trends in jewellery design. The modern jewellery exhibition which he staged at Goldsmiths' Hall made 1961 a climactic year for the young British jeweller. Originally planned with a budget of seven thousand pounds it dawned on Hughes as the exhibits rolled in from all over the world that this was to be an event of more than ordinary significance. As the range and scope of the exhibition grew so the cost escalated, eventually coming to rest at a horrifying twenty-two thousand pounds.

Artists like Mary Kessel, Elizabeth Frink and Robert Adams were sent a little box of wax and asked to produce a model. Andrew Grima at the H. J. Company was then commissioned to cast them into jewels for the exhibition, the intention being to exploit them in a limited edition afterwards. Although they made an attractive contribution to the exhibition it is generally agreed that most of these pieces were too heavy to be a commercial success. Nevertheless, the exhibition was a triumph and it would be difficult to exaggerate its importance.

Freedom was what the new movement was about, but that did not mean that because inhibition was discarded, discipline went out with the bathwater. Random although these designs may appear, the best of them have an organic coherence which gives them mechanical as well as aesthetic strength. Although superficially it appears as though in some of these designs the different elements have been thrown into the air and allowed to fall where they will, each is in fact carefully related to the whole. Some explode from a central point or implode towards it; others are parallel as slanting hail or windblown sand. There are strong connections here with the *objet trouvé* which so fascinated us at the time—the found object which owes its shape to chance or the work of nature.

The crystals which so many young jewellers used in their work were literally *objets trouvés*. David Thomas even remembers picking them up from the ground while on holiday in Cornwall. Certainly a visitor to the white-washed vaults of Gregory Bottley, the mineral dealers in Kensington Church Street, might have met any one of half a dozen jewellers. Unlike many trends in jewellery design the fashion for rough crystals does not seem to have come from a single innovator but to have arisen from the extraordinary melting pot of ideas which was on the boil at the time.[1]

1. Against this Andrew Grima has suggested that the idea may have been initiated and spread by an enterprising salesman hawking minerals from South America.

The Sixties

The idea was not entirely new: Roman emeralds often show the six-sided form of the original crystal and in the Renaissance it was fashionable to wear a natural octahedron of diamond in a ring. Rough aquamarines appear in Edward Spencer's Golden Fleece necklace and Sah Oved set a crystal of citrine in a pendant long before the idea became fashionable. The obsession with rough crystals was certainly very closely connected with South Kensington, and the nearness of the Royal College of Art to the Geological Museum may well have had something to do with it.

DAVID THOMAS

David Thomas (born 1938) studied metalwork at Twickenham School of Art between 1952 and 1957 when he won a scholarship which enabled him to study in Italy and France. During 1958 and 1959 he was working with the historic firm of Bolin, Swedish crown jewellers and in former days jewellers to the Russian Imperial crown. He finished his studies in Kensington.

In 1959 life for a student at the Royal College could be frustrating as well as exciting. Jewellery was regarded as little more than the handmaiden of the fashion department and it was fashion jewellery that was looked for. To this end the workshops were stocked with drawer upon drawer of flashing pastes and stamped-gilt galleries and settings. Not surprisingly much of Thomas's output at this time was in the base metals. He soon discovered his natural empathy for gold, however, and set up a workshop in his parents' home in Hampton, moving to his present establishment in Chelsea in 1965

Unlike the jewellers of the Arts and Crafts movement, Thomas has a passion for machines and invents or adapts gadgets to help him in his work whenever he sees the chance: his great regret is that jewellery employs such simple methods that these opportunities are few and far between. Some of Thomas's most characteristic jewels are formed from a tracery of gold wire which is soldered with a micro-welder. These are far too intricate to be designed by putting pencil to paper and Thomas simply makes them up as he goes along. Light and surprisingly strong, with the little globules formed by the micro-welder at each joint exerting considerable eye appeal, they are successful jewels in every way. This approach is typical, as he firmly believes that the object should grow out of the materials and that too much reliance on drawings can mislead and deceive.

Another technique which David Thomas evolved was that of embedding wires in the wax pattern of an investment casting. This allowed jewels to be produced in limited numbers but with all the detail and finish of an individually made piece (Plate 106).

Thomas came to rough crystals with his contemporaries at a time when they were

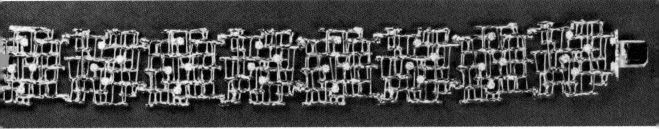

Courtesy of the Worshipful Company of Goldsmiths

106. Gold and diamond BRACELET *by* DAVID THOMAS

cheap and plentiful and used them through the sixties (Colour Plate XVIId). In a pendant of 1968, for example, he spreads an airburst of splintered gold around a knot of quartz crystals and spatters it with golden droplets (Plate 107), an idea he also adapted to other jewels.

His intriguing Master's Badge for the Grocers' Company has an outer border formed from a mosaic of spice seeds. The idea was a boyishly romantic one intended, with the little camel in the coat of arms, to suggest the caravan bringing its cargo of cloves, peppers, cardamoms and corianders from fragrant grove to clamourous market. Thomas used real spices bought from an Indian shop to make the mould and remembers well the piquant whiff of the orient that came off the investment when the molten metal was poured.

Forms in his earlier years were unmistakably organic and often seem to have been derived from sea creatures: barnacles or starfish or nameless organisms from the

107. PENDANT *of gold, quartz crystals and garnets by* DAVID THOMAS

hundred-fathom mark, all corally encrustation and glistening diamond-tipped papillae (Plate 108). The Atlantis collection was designed by Thomas to be made in a limited edition by Prestige Jewellery Ltd using his own methods, and it was an instant success.

As time went on his work became more architectural and ultimately, in the new collection of 1974, purely mathematical. The jewels of the new collection do not simply represent shapes, but express with the violent explicitness of the film cartoonist, movement, development and transmutation. Lines delight and elude the eye by dodging back upon themselves or writhing in the eternal journey of the

Courtesy of the Worshipful Company of
Goldsmiths

108. (left) A gold, sapphire and diamond RING *designed by* DAVID THOMAS *and made by* PRESTIGE JEWELLERY *(enlarged)*

109. (right) Yellow topaz, gold and diamond RING *by* DAVID THOMAS, *1975 (enlarged)*

Mobius band. A smooth gold ring suddenly expands and delaminates like the pages of a book in a manner both pleasing and disconcerting (Plate 109). A pair of domed earstuds has an oval area scooped out on each side in contoured layers like the tide-scoured grain in a piece of driftwood; as the jewel is turned you can suddenly see right through it and realize that the pattern has been made like the louvres of a blind. Thomas likes jewels you can see into: sometimes what appears to be thin engraved lines are slots pierced à jour. The new collection is full of such surprises and discoveries.

Much of this series is in traditionally finished gold and pavé-set diamonds, but there is nothing orthodox about it and nothing sterile either. Neither is it as unconnected as one might suppose from his earlier organic designs, and the geometry of the new collection is the shifting, subtly delighting symmetry of a seashell or a chrysalis.

JOHN DONALD

John Donald (born 1928) began by studying graphic art at Farnham and came to jewellery later at the Royal College of Art. He benefited early from the Goldsmiths' patronage by winning a competition for the Company's badges and subsequently making them.

Donald was among the first to experiment with crystals. With no knowledge of mineralogy it was a painful process of trial and error and brilliant successes were balanced by absurd failures. Many of the most beautiful crystals turned out to be either soluble or else so brittle that as soon as he tried to grind them down to reduce size and weight they crumbled to pieces. Nevertheless, Donald had a great gift for this kind of work, and these early mounts for rough gems are so apt as to appear like an extension of the crystal matrix.

At the same time Donald was exploring ways of treating the precious metals. Heat is essential to the making of jewellery and the use, and even misuse, of the flame can produce a wide range of effects and textures. Fabergé, the Russian court jeweller, was probably the first to extend the use of the flame beyond its purpose of softening, soldering and casting metal. Sheet silver was heated to a point just short of melting when it wrinkled into an agreeable nugetty texture. The sheet was then cut up and made into cigarette boxes. Fabergé called his technique *samorodok*. Heat a fragment of silver or 18-carat gold and it first glows red, then appears to exude a glistening sweat. Cooling at this point results in Fabergé's *samorodok* effect. Heat it still further and it rolls into a spinning quicksilver globule of molten metal.

Donald was intrigued by the splashes of solder made by the plumber when wiping a joint in lead pipe and he attempted to reproduce the same effect in 18-carat gold by pouring the metal on the workshop floor. The results were disconcerting: instead of spreading in a gleaming web on hitting the ground it burst into myriad tiny drops which flew into the furthest cranny of the workshop. Only a fraction of it was ever found. He next tried pouring molten gold into water and the result of this, although just as unexpected, was more promising. He was left with an assortment of fascinating shapes: most were flattish and irregular like cornflakes; some were the expected spherical shot and others were formed into a tiny cup by a pocket of steam. The cup and ball motifs Donald used in a whole range of successful jewels and they became a characteristic of his work (Plate 110).

Chenier, small-bore tubing supplied from stock by the bullion merchants, was used by him in the most ingenious ways. Lengths of it were laid side by side in an

110. *Jewels by* JOHN DONALD *including: a gold cup and ball* BRACELET; *a gold and diamond drum* BROOCH *(bottom left); a pair of gold and malachite* EARCLIPS *(top right); a gold and diamond* RING *(left); a gold and baroque pearl* RING *(centre)*

organpipe effect. Square cheniers he sliced off diagonally and then arranged around a central gem like an exploding firework (Colour Plate XVIIb). One such brooch has a candy-sugar cluster of dark-brown citrines at its centre, and the sectioned tips of the cheniers which sprout from it are burnished into diamond-shaped scintilla contrasting with the rough-finished sides of the tubes.

In many of Donald's jewels the setting echoes the idea of crystals (Plate 111): a wulfenite group framed with a random trelliswork of gold as though it had grown with the tabular crystals of some secondary mineral as so often happens in nature (Colour Plate XVIIc), or white quartz enclosed by gold prisms capped with diamonds.

Donald's self-styled 'drum brooch' is a clever design which allows diamonds to be set on fine stalks without fear of damage (Plate 110). A ring of gold encloses the design and from it diamonds grow inwards towards the open centre on slender filaments. Like the great majority of his designs it is of natural origin, suggesting the section through a grass stem or a fish's eye view of its pond, although even Donald cannot say where the idea came from in the first place. As with so many of his contemporaries Donald's jewels owe much to nature without attempting to imitate it.

One of the mistakes of the nineteenth-century jeweller was his attempt to make perfect copies of flowers, birds and insects in gold, silver and diamonds. Only a handful of Parisian jewellers were successful at it and even the most brilliant of

111. A gold and iron-pyrites BROOCH, *by* JOHN DONALD, *the setting reflecting the cubic form of the crystals*

Massin's roses seems to exude a faint odour of wax and embalming fluid. A sparrow's feather or a snowflake are unique and inimitable and no jeweller should attempt to copy them precisely.

GERDA FLOCKINGER

In 1961 a course in experimental jewellery was begun at Hornsey School of Art under the direction of Gerda Flockinger. Born in Innsbruck, Austria in 1927 she came to this country in 1938 and studied at St Martin's School of Art and the Central. The course was a brilliant success and was to have considerable influence on design in the later sixties and early seventies. Emphasis was on design rather than on technique which the student was expected to learn at the Sir John Cass School in Whitechapel.

In her early work Gerda Flockinger experimented with enamels and rough gems. Later she came to rely more and more on the flame and on fusion techniques, arriving at an intensely original style which she has been refining and maturing ever since. Nowadays she uses cabochon gems which she cuts herself and coral cameos of which she acquired a parcel some years ago. These she uses not only for their textural quality but for themselves, and their ruddy little faces windowed in her jewels add to their curiously elfin quality. Untroubled by fashionable inhibitions about using diamonds, she does not hesitate to set them in her work whenever the design calls for it, white, and sometimes coloured stones, lightly dewing the crusty gold and silver surfaces essential to her style.

There has been a feeling among some younger jewellers that to use diamonds in jewellery is to exploit the African miners who produced them. Apart from the fact that diamonds are mined in other parts of Africa besides the Republic, and other parts of the world besides Africa, such an argument would make life impossible if

125

carried to its logical conclusion. Gerda herself has been heard to say that there are two kinds of jewellers, those who make jewellery and those who talk about it. By its very nature much of her work is extemporized as she goes along. She does make drawings, however, literally hundreds of them, exquisitely detailed in sepia ink. Insisting upon making everything with her own hands she will not employ an assistant and is acutely conscious that there are not enough days in the year for her to make everything she would like. As a result the drawings have become a finite creative end in themselves.

The actual jewels, rings like the case of a caddis worm, medallions and necklace links like blobs of waterborn foam seem not merely to have been inspired by nature but to have been shaped by the forces of creation themselves.

The elements of her jewels are fused together, the method being to paint them with flux and then heat them to the point of melting when they sweat out a shimmering deliquescent coating. There is perfection in the very asymmetry of her jewels: no single part of any one of them is a pair or an exact match with any other part yet everything is under absolute control. Needless to say, she never repeats a jewel. Basically two-dimensional, emphasis and contrast in her work came from lightly encrusted low-relief scrolls and snail tracks of melted wire or minute balls of precious metal. Originally these tiny clusters served the secondary purpose of concealing a joint, but the decorative function eventually obscured the practical till they now spawn in glistening clusters like golden caviar.

112. *Two silver* RINGS *by* GERDA FLOCKINGER *set with a Persian turquoise intaglio* (left), *and an Indian carved emerald* (right)

113. A BRACELET *of silver and pearls by* GERDA FLOCKINGER

Movement is important in her work and she supplies it with a variety of drops and pendants: slender paillons of fused metal, shimmering fringes of baroque pearls tipped with burnished 'bootlace tags' and, most characteristically, long rods wrapped with half-melted spirals like thread around a bobbin (Plate 112). Many of her jewels are set with pearls, sometimes coloured, natural freshwater pearls from Lake Biwa in Japan, but usually cultured baroque pearls, often stained to a silvery grey. Machine-made chain is never seen in her jewels: necklace links are pierced out of flat sheet or formed of a coil of wire—she has also made some delightful rings by the latter method.

A few years ago she began to open up her work à jour, letting the light through eyelets and spirals, to bring to it a note of tension (Plate 113). Now the mood of her jewels seems to be changing again, and one senses in them a new compactness, precision and delicacy.

CHARLES DE TEMPLE

Charles de Temple is an American who chooses to live and work in London. He had no formal artistic training and began by selling jewels of his own making to the Paris fashion houses. They were simple ornaments in gilt silver and semi-precious stones, but effective for the way in which they contrasted rough and bland surfaces. At this stage he was literally learning as he went along by trial and error and his technical shortcomings were painfully brought home to him when his jewels were returned because soldered joints had failed. From here he moved on to what he called his 'nervous jewels', prickly designs in two-coloured gold wire.

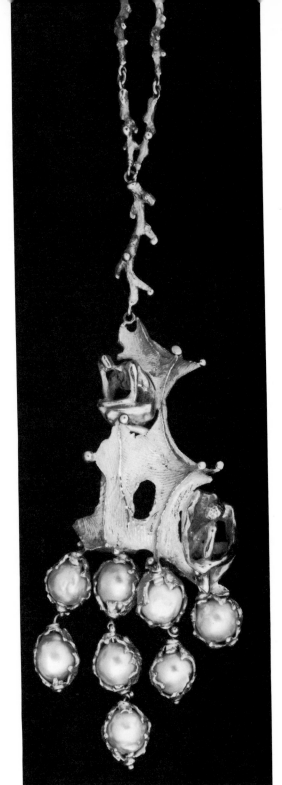

114. (above) *A gold and ruby-crystal* BROOCH *by* CHARLES DE TEMPLE *the flower petals textured with the flame*

115. (right) *A gold* PENDANT, *by* CHARLES DE TEMPLE, *cast from a model made by pouring wax into the closed fist, and hung with cultured pearls*

In these early days de Temple made every mistake that it is possible for a young designer to make. He designed a pair of earrings in the style of Calder and sold the idea to Bloomingdales—who promptly ordered two and a half gross. He had already made half a dozen pairs before reluctantly coming to the conclusion that it was not a practical proposition. He too used natural crystals in his work (Plate 114), but discovered that the unique, one-off quality which held their principal appeal also made it impossible to use them in even the most limited edition of repeats.

De Temple feels that he owes much to Lalique and Dali and many of his jewels do have a melting, stretching quality—squiggling droplets appear in some of them. De Temple's favourite fantasy is that his jewels are the artifacts of some immeasurably ancient civilization, an Atlantis of the soul, lost before it even existed and which only he can unearth. Be that as it may, his jewels are well made, original, and easy to wear (Plate 115).

HUBERT TAYLOR ROSE

Hubert Taylor Rose (born 1909), is almost entirely self-taught, his formal artistic training limited to a correspondence course he took as a boy. His first job was at Austin Reed's, 'passing the pins' in the display department. He had already joined the Honourable Artillery Company when war broke out but ended up in 'R Force' an élite camouflage unit whose job was not merely to conceal what was there so much as to convince the enemy it was still there when in fact it had moved somewhere else. With him in the same unit were Basil Spence, John Hutton, Stephen Sykes and Tom Ladell. After the war he returned to Austin Reed where he eventually became director in charge of building operations.

The idea of making jewellery was first suggested to him by an Italian diplomat he met at a dinner party who made it for a pastime. Then, on a visit to the Central School of Art in search of display talent, he saw the jewellery students at work and decided to enrol for the evening classes. At that time, in the mid-fifties, instruction was stilted and uninspired. For example, as an exercise students were given a piece of copper and a piece of brass; they were asked to cut an identical pattern out of each and then inlay the one into the other.

Taylor Rose still has a lapis lazuli and silver necklace he made at this time and recalls how he was given the design for it and then told how to proceed every step of the way. The design was one of sennit knots and strongly recalls the Guild of Handicrafts: clearly the dead hand of the Arts and Crafts movement still weighed heavily on some art schools at this time. After three months he decided he would be better off teaching himself and looking back now he realizes that most of what he learned came from books.

116. A silver PENDANT *by* HUBERT TAYLOR ROSE

Hubert Taylor Rose is a great admirer of the Bauhaus and their influence is very apparent in the strength and simplicity of his work. He is best known for bold openwork designs, grid-like patterns made, not with the piercing-saw, but by laying slabs of silver side by side and soldering them (Plate 116). Other jewels are in stepped geometrical designs, clearly of Mexican inspiration (Plate 117).

Cabochons of black onyx figure in his work and here the story is the usual one of his having come by a parcel of these stones (Plate 118). He had also used uncut crystals of iron pyrites which he bought in, of all places, a barber's shop on the island of Elba. His output was limited to about six pieces a year and he remains an amateur in the best and purest sense of the word. Never has he sold a single piece of jewellery and this freedom from the constraints of commerce has allowed him to experiment and explore every possibility that took his fancy. Examples of his work are in the Goldsmiths' Hall collection.

GILLIAN PACKARD

Gillian Packard (born 1938) studied at Kingston School of Art, the Central, and finally at the Royal College. Much of her early work was in enamel, and in fact her entry in the 1962 exhibition was a necklace of enamel on copper. Soon afterwards

130

117. A silver COLLAR *by* HUBERT TAYLOR ROSE

118. A silver and onyx BRACELET *by* HUBERT TAYLOR ROSE

119. *(left) Gold* RINGS *set with semi-precious stones by* GILLIAN PACKARD
120. *(above) Two 18-carat gold and diamond combined wedding and engagement* RINGS *by* GILLIAN PACKARD

she turned towards 18-carat gold and the semi-precious stones and is probably best known for her rings (Plate 119). Not only is the ring the most popular kind of jewel, but the built-in limitations imposed upon it by the way it is worn pose a challenge and a conundrum to the designer. Gillian Packard's rings are deft, attractive and wearable. Some are designed so that the engagement ring fits into the wedding band like an old puzzle ring (Plate 120); others kink and twist and loop like amorous eels.

Gillian Packard's jewels are seen at their best in wear, particularly her earrings. One of the most successful designs is a sort of penman's flourish of gold punctuated with a single diamond and with a little spherule of gold at the tip so that it can be poked painlessly through the pierced ear. The effect is that of a stray lock of 18-carat gold hair (Plate 121). A pendant like a silver branch hung with cornelian pears seems to have strayed from some twilight tale of Bran or Cuchulain.

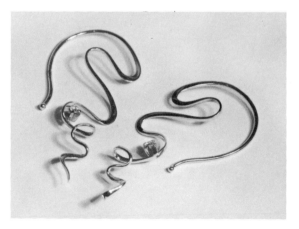

121. *A pair of 18-carat gold and diamond* EARRINGS *by* GILLIAN PACKARD

Her designs range from the mythical to the mathematical but in all of them apparent simplicity masks inner complexity. Most of them are readily adaptable for reproduction in limited quantities but a great deal of her time is still taken up by private commissions.

NEVIN HOLMES

Nevin Holmes (born Princess Konitsa, 1928) is the daughter of a Turkish ambassador. She trained as a concert pianist and then studied painting and etching at the Central from 1958 to 1962. Her first jewels were made in 1960 and she is perhaps best known for her massive gold rings set with big cabochons of emerald, pink tourmaline, lapis lazuli and star-sapphire beads and baroque pearls (Plates 122, 123). Her approach is instinctive and non-intellectual, arising from a deep

122 and 123. 18-carat gold RINGS *set with pearls and semi-precious stones by* NEVIN HOLMES

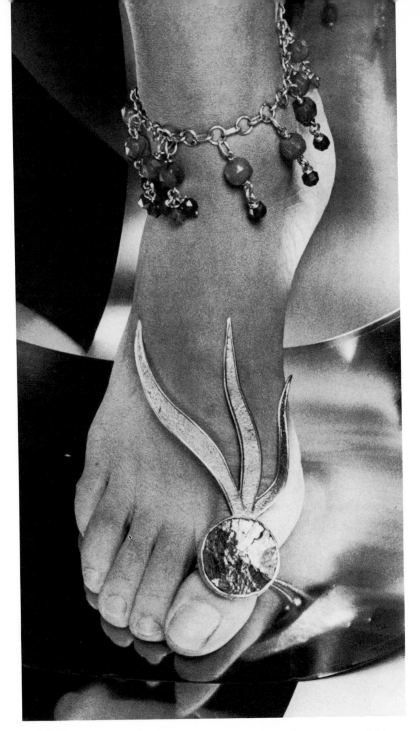

124. *An 18-carat gold and uncut ruby* TOE RING *and an* ANKLET *of 18-carat gold and cornelian beads by* NEVIN HOLMES *(reduced)*

understanding of precious metal, a passion for colour and a strong sense of theatre. Without being in any sense derivative her work is powerfully Byzantine in mood as though her jewels were the regalia in some ageless Trapezuntine ritual. Prodigal of materials she uses masses of 18-carat gold and makes what she feels like—garters, toe rings or huge necklaces for men (Plate 124). She tends to avoid raw, shining metal because a mirror-like surface puts up a barrier between the wearer and the essential nature of precious metal.

STEWART DEVLIN

Stewart Devlin (born 1931) is an Australian by birth who came to the Royal College of Art on a scholarship in 1960. During 1963 and 1964 he designed the new Australian decimal coinage, and the lines of communication which this opened up with the Royal Mint and the Goldsmiths' Company strengthened his connections with London. Almost inevitably he opened a workshop here in 1965.

In these early days he was known principally as a silversmith and his work has been characterized by what has been called filigree—patterns of openwork reticulation. When he decided to make jewellery this idea of complex openwork was carried into it, especially in his 'cariatic' designs (Plate 126). At a glance these appear to be in random openwork, but a closer look shows them to be made of tiny, naked human figures dancing in procession as a bracelet, playing ring-a-roses as a wedding band, or scrambling in a human pyramid on each other's shoulders as pendent earrings.

125. *A gold and pearl* BROOCH *by* STEWART DEVLIN

126. *A gold 'cariatic'* BROOCH *by* STEWART DEVLIN

127. *Gold* EASTER EGGS *by* STEWART DEVLIN

There has been something of a cult for Devlin's Easter eggs, each of which opens to reveal a surprise in the form of a gem crystal or a flower (Plate 127).

EMANUEL RAFT

Another Australian, born in 1938 of Italian Greek parents, Emanuel Raft seems to owe more to the Mediterranean than the Anglo-Saxon tradition. He began by studying architecture and moved on to sculpture and painting. His first one-man show of jewellery was mounted in 1963.

His earlier jewels in cast silver and roughly knapped opal bear the powerful imprint of natural textures like wood or tidal sand (Plate 128). In the 1970s form began to take over from texture. Accurately cut gems were slotted or clipped into these witty designs of folded metal in ways that are simple as well as secure. Often in the exotic metals like zirconium or titanium they look as though they could be stripped down and reassembled like a gun (Plate 129).

Raft's work has now moved into a third, quite different phase. There is a literary element in these little visual wisecracks: a torn scrap of silver attached to a lapis lazuli heart, suggesting a love letter, or the splintered fragment of a door, hinges and all.

LOUIS OSMAN

Louis Osman (born 1914) is an architect by education and training. He studied drawing at the Slade and during 1936 and 1937 was with the British Museum and British School of Archaeology expeditions to Syria.

Osman's approach is brusque and direct. Fragments of ruby as rough as when they

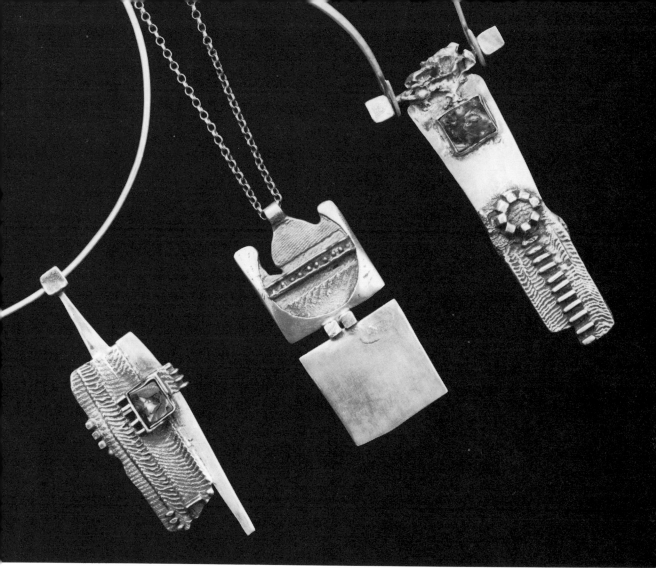

128. Three PENDANTS *in cast silver and black opal by* EMANUEL RAFT

129. RING *set with a cornelian by*
EMANUEL RAFT

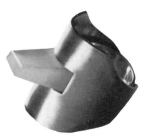

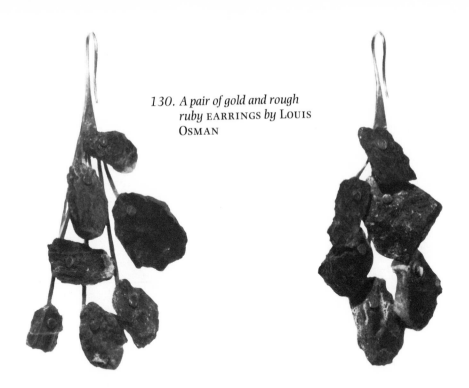

130. A pair of gold and rough ruby EARRINGS *by* LOUIS OSMAN

left the ground are riveted to branches of gold as huge pendent earrings, and the hooks which secure them to the ear are turned aggressively to the front (Plate 130). A chain of hammered links is hung with knobbly baroque cultured pearls (Plate 131), a torc is fashioned extempore from thin, crumpled gold sheet. Osman's best-known work is the crown given by the Goldsmiths' Company for the investiture of HRH The Prince of Wales.

DESMOND CLEN MURPHY

Desmond Clen Murphy (born 1924) is perhaps better known as a silversmith than as a jeweller. His approach to the setting of rough crystals is uncomplicated but original and his rough-hewn treatment of gold and silver never lets one forget that they too are of the earth. His treatment is monolithic, the setting simple, sometimes minimal, but invariably apt and going with the complex visual grain of the stone.

131. A gold and cultured-pearl CHAIN *by* LOUIS OSMAN

FRANCES BECK and ERNEST BLYTH

The close, working partnerships which flourished in the old Arts and Crafts days are uncommon now. Frances Beck and Ernest Blyth work so closely together that their two individual styles have merged into one. Frances Beck (born 1939) was a graduate of Glasgow Art School. Her delicate designs are characterized by whorls and undulations which keep the eye in constant movement. This quality of movement is important in her designs, some of which appear to be melting like wax, an illusion helped by liquid-like droplets hung tremulously *en pampille* as though about to fall splashing down at any second (Plate 132).

Ernest Blyth (born 1939) was an apprentice assayer at Goldsmiths' Hall and learnt the rudiments of his silversmithing part-time at the Central School of Arts and Crafts. The Hall subsidized the cost of the metal but even so he found it expensive. Apart from the cost of working relatively large pieces of silver, the noise in a home workshop can be pretty intimidating. Silversmiths' tools and equipment are bulky and take up a lot of space so that it was in the nature of things that he should have gravitated towards jewellery. His designs tend to be robust and linear, composed of flats and angles.

It was while working for Andrew Grima that he met Frances Beck and they began

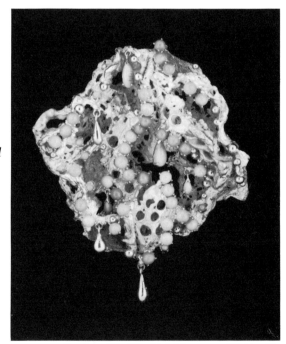

132. *A* BROOCH *in 18-carat yellow gold and turquoise by* BLYTH *and* BECK

Courtesy of the Worshipful Company of Goldsmiths

their successful partnership. More recently they have been experimenting with contrasting coloured golds—one sheet of gold sweated to another and then chiselled through to expose the different tints of metal.

ANDREW GRIMA

Andrew Grima was born in Rome in 1921 and came to England with his family at the age of five. He studied engineering at Nottingham university and served with the Royal Engineers in India and Burma during the Second World War.

When he was demobbed in 1946 Grima, like so many other young servicemen, found himself with no very clear sense of direction. He gravitated into the jewellery business almost fortuitously when he married Helen Haller, the daughter of a manufacturing jeweller in 1947. Grima's father-in-law specialized in cast jewels for export to Latin America and South Africa until import restrictions overseas and the crippling rate of British purchase tax obliged them to turn towards the renovating and restyling of old jewels. Andrew took over the business when his father-in-law died in 1951.

In the early fifties he made an exclusive agreement with Michael Gottschalk and they were very successful, making and selling jewels in direct competition with the Italians who were attempting to saturate the British market at this time. When Gottschalk moved to the South of France in 1963 Grima began working with the newly formed firm of Hooper Bolton and it was this which gave him the chance he needed to design jewels for the smart, intelligent, newly independent woman of the sixties.

By this time he had formulated his own clear and individual ideas about what jewellery was and ought to be. On the negative side he felt a growing abhorrence for jewels whose only function was to show off the gems with which they were set and which were distinguished only by their anonymity. He had no use for platinum whose only virtue that he could see was that it was exceedingly expensive. Generally he preferred 18-carat yellow gold but where a silvery finish was essential, for example in the pavé-setting of diamonds, he favoured the new white-gold alloys. Grima wanted to make big jewels that were daring, fantastic, even flamboyant but without being clumsy or brash (Plate 133).

Economics as well as personal taste ousted large rubies, diamonds, emeralds and sapphires from his palette and replaced them to a large degree with tourmalines, peridots, opals, aquamarines and topaz. Grima was never so dogmatic as to abandon them altogether, but when he used large emeralds they tended to be light, bright and inexpensive, and sapphires to be of the Cambridge-blue Ceylon variety. Carved Indian stones were not only cheap but brought a certain exotic tang to a jewel

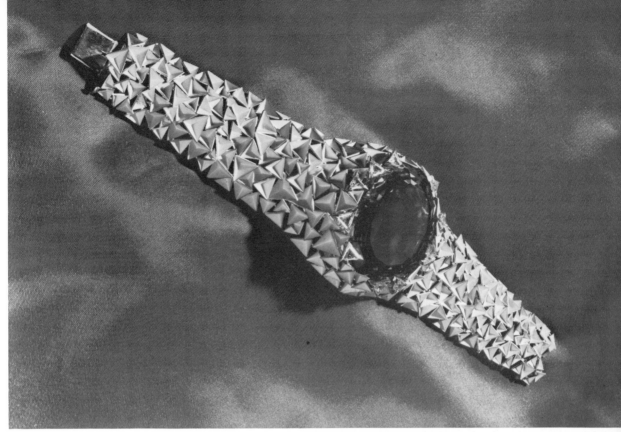

133. An 18-carat gold, amethyst and diamond BRACELET *by* ANDREW GRIMA

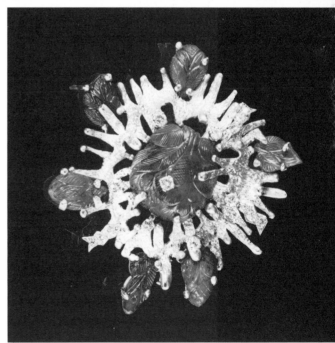

134. An Indian carved ruby, diamond and gold BROOCH *by* ANDREW GRIMA

135. *A gold and diamond* COLLAR *by* ANDREW GRIMA

(Plate 134). Far from making do without diamonds, on the other hand, he insisted that at least one be included in every design as a foil to the warm yellow of the gold or an antidote to the richness of a coloured stone (Colour Plate XVIIe). In fact something like half of Grima's jewels by number are just of gold and diamonds.

Inevitably Grima was among those who set uncut minerals as gems. He was particularly intrigued by those swirling nodules of grey agate that look as though they have been stirred up with a stick. A brooch in the Goldsmiths' Hall collection is set with one of these stones in the midst of a viper's nest of wriggling gold and diamond tentacles (Colour Plate XVIIa).

One of Grima's most successful effects was obtained by soldering wires side by side and then working a texture into the reeded surface (Plate 135). This simple device was used to create a variety of moods and effects: arranged horizontally in a brooch with slivers of pavé-set diamond and the impression is of sunlit water; fashioned as a meandering bracelet of jagged peaks with topazes and diamonds and it resembles the frenetic doodlings of a lie detector; arrange the wire radially and we have the star of some lunatic order of chivalry.

142

The collection of watches which he designed for Omega was perhaps his most extraordinary venture. The series was christened 'About Time' and comprised eighty-six pieces: fifty watches and thirty-one matching jewels. There were bracelets, clips, rings, even pill boxes, but one theme united them all: the watch face was either seen through a precious stone or concealed by one. The designs were fantastic, sometimes to the point of magnificent impracticality. 'Tornado', for example, was a massive coil of gold wire streaked with diamonds, the glass of limpid venus-hair stone shot through with crystals of golden rutile. It weighed half a pound. 'About Time' travelled the world and sales were based on the principle of total exclusivity: as soon as a design was sold it was replaced with another different one. Omega have now followed through with a range of watches factory-made to their own specifications but based on Grima's designs.

The fantasy that Grima pours into his jewels seems to spill over into his surroundings. Seeing the rocky exterior of his shop for the first time one might be forgiven for thinking that a rogue asteroid had left its orbit and embedded itself in the Portland stone and gold leaf of Jermyn Street. Inside, the interplanetary illusion is made complete by a magnificent spiral staircase of clear acrylic and the curved showcases which, instead of housing Martian plant cultures, protect even rarer creatures of gold, zoisite, diamond and chalcedony.

It is interesting that so little enamel jewellery was made in the sixties. Colour there was in plenty, lavishly supplied by rough crystals, but few jewellers practised this demanding craft. Gillian Packard and Gerda Flockinger experimented with enamel in their early years, only to abandon it later, and Thelma Robertson's delightful collar, although quite in harmony with the naturalism of the time, was a brilliant exception (Colour Plate XVIII).

Change in the sixties went beyond a mere shift in fashion; the whole attitude to jewellery had changed. Vyvyan Holland writes of the unwritten sumptuary laws which prevailed in his youth: 'No gentleman in a morning coat could carry a parcel, however small, and all forms of jewellery were forbidden, the most that could be allowed being one or two pearls in the dress suit and gold cufflinks. A pearl tiepin could be worn but no diamonds.'[2] A bookmaker or a publican was permitted to wear a tiepin and a diamond ring, but in any other British male the wearing of jewellery was regarded as unwholesome and even tinged with perversion.

Superintendent Arthur Askew's impressions of Maundy Gregory, the notorious purveyor of honours are revealing: 'There was an air of the bogus about him. He was too well dressed, used too much oil in his hair, wore too many rings—one, a green

2. Vyvyan Holland, *Time Remembered*, 1966.

scarab ring had belonged to Oscar Wilde, so he said. I said to myself, Hello, here's a crook if ever I saw one.'[3]

Aleister Crowley, mountaineer and self-styled poet and magician, habitually loaded himself with rings, bracelets, earrings and pendants and was even observed to be wearing a large topaz ring during the ascent of K2. Today it is hard to imagine the horror and revulsion which the 'Great Beast', shaven headed and with rings hung in his pierced ears, must have inspired in his day. His appearance in Bond Street today would scarcely occasion more than a second glance.

The wearing of jewellery by men was one of the many taboos that disappeared in the sixties. Unisex had arrived and with it jewellery for men. Shoulder-length hair discouraged the wearing of earrings—that lay ahead in the crop-haired seventies— but there were massive identity-bracelets of gold curb-linking and all manner of neckgear from the hippies strings of wooden beads to luxurious creations of high-carat gold and precious stones.

A polo-necked jumper of silk or cashmere provided an ideal background for a string of beads or a silver chain for the party-going male and even quite senior citizens were to be seen wearing a pendant of carved Chinese jade. Rings were no longer restricted to the signet with its engraved crest or initials but were made in a multiplicity of designs and crammed on every finger. The peacock male had returned and it took a world depression to chase him out of the sunlight.

It was freedom above all which characterized the sixties, freedom to do what you fancied—to 'do your own thing' as we said at the time. Occasionally we abused our freedom, the jeweller as much as the rest of us. The best of the new designers kicked off the encumbrances of stale tradition and set off to find, not just a new source of inspiration but a new discipline, a new kind of symmetry, a mould to contain, shape and solidify its abundant fluid energy. Those who found the first without the second not only failed themselves but did much to push the style into the hands of costume jewellers and cheap mass-manufacturers. They juggled endlessly with textures and surfaces without ever realizing that to give them structure and coherence would take a skill and a subtlety that was beyond them.

Much remains to us still from this exciting if hysterical decade long after the Carnaby Street clothes have disintegrated in the twin tub—long even after the Arabs turned the tap on cheap oil and easy prosperity. The economic depression of the early seventies sobered and tempered our attitudes, but the habits of experimentation and enquiry still remain and above all there are richer opportunities of learning the craft in our art schools than ever before.

3. Tom Cullen, *Maundy Gregory Purveyor of Honours*, 1974.

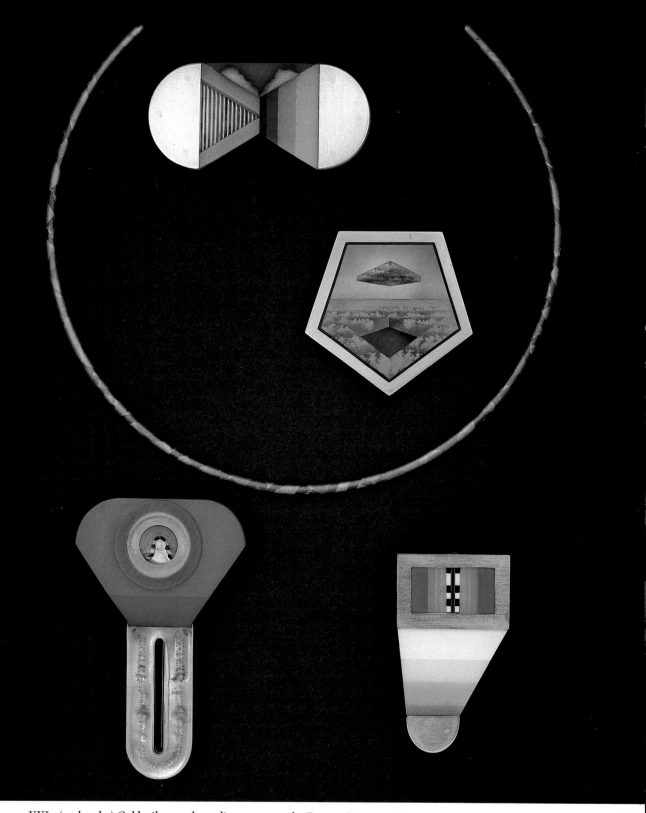

XXI. *(a, d and e) Gold, silver and acrylic* BROOCHES *by* ROGER MORRIS. See page 150
(b) Silver and titanium dreamscape BROOCH *by* EDWARD DE LARGE. See page 146
(c) Titanium TORC *by* EDWARD DE LARGE. See page 148

XXII.   *(a)* *Silver and dyed-acrylic* PENDANT *by* NUALA JAMIESON. See page 154
        (b) *Dyed-acrylic* BANGLE *by* NUALA JAMIESON. See page 154
        (c and f) *Dyed-acrylic* RINGS *by* NUALA JAMIESON. See page 154
        (d) *Silver, wood and dyed-nylon* BANGLE *by* CAROLINE BROADHEAD. See page 170
        (e) *Silver spool* RING *wound with nylon filament by* CAROLINE BROADHEAD.

XXIII. *(a and b) Silver and enamel multiple* RINGS *on bronze holders, by* WENDY RAMSHAW.
See page 156
(c) Gem-set gold multiple RINGS *on perspex holder, by* WENDY RAMSHAW.
See page 156
(d) A gold and acrylic plastic BANGLE *by* DAVID WATKINS. See page 156
(e) A two-colour gold BANGLE *by* DAVID WATKINS.

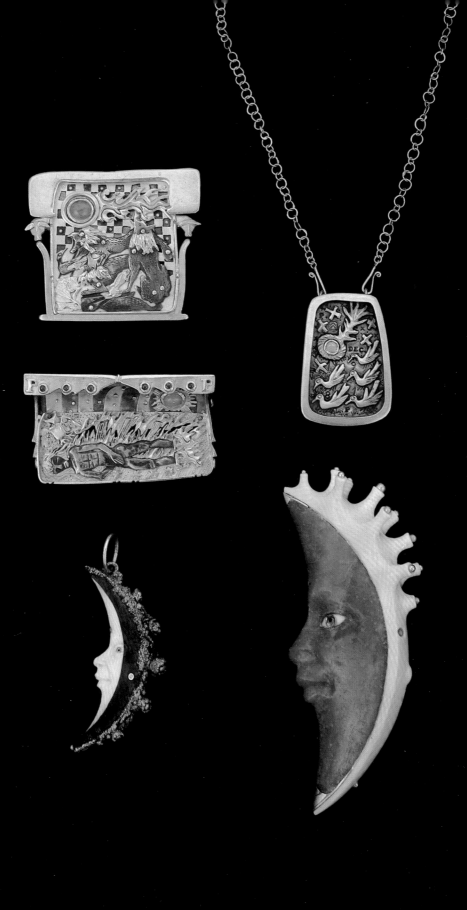

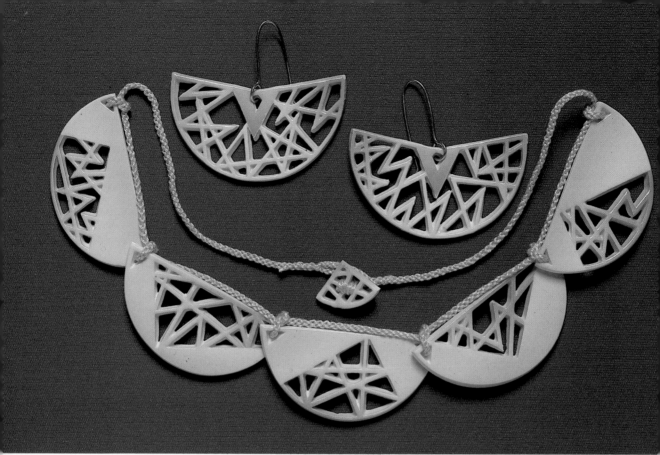

XXVI. *A bone-china* NECKLACE *and* EARRINGS *by* AILEEN HAMILTON. See page 176

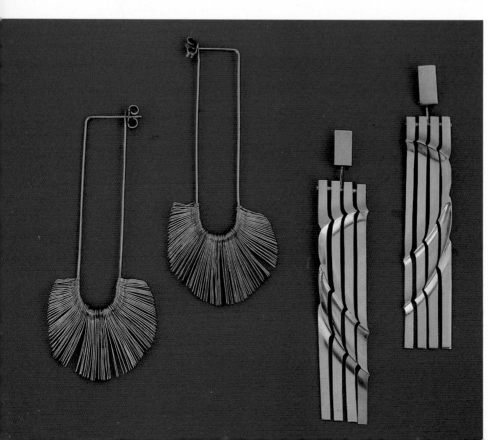

XXVII. (a) *A pair of platinum and gold* EARRINGS *by* SALLY DRIVER. See page 175
(b) *A pair of platinum and gold* EARRINGS *by* DEBORAH COWIN. See page 160 *Both 1982 Platinum Award winners*

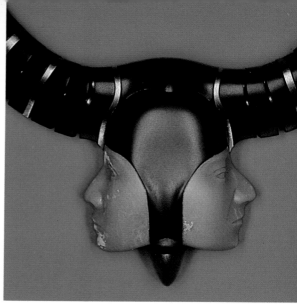

XXVIII. *(a) A* COLLAR *in white gold, nephrite, crystal and opal by* CHARLOTTE DE SYLLAS *(reduced)*
See page 179

(b) Detail of the front of the same jewel (enlarged)

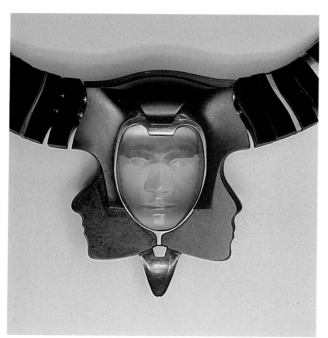

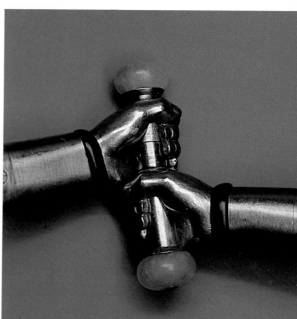

(c) Detail of the reverse (enlarged)

(d) The clasp of the collar (enlarged)

XXIX. (overleaf) *Ephemeral jewels.* See pages 181–5
    (a) EARRING *in screened acrylic by* GEOFF ROBERTS.
    (b) BROOCH *of inlaid wood by* PETER NICZEWSKI.
    (c) EARRING *in screened acrylic by* GEOFF ROBERTS.
    (d) BRACELET *in dyed acrylic by* HILARY BROWN.
    (e) BROOCH *in screened acrylic by* ALISON BAXTER.
    (f) COLLAR *in polythene and acrylic by* ALISON BAXTER.
    (g) BRACELET *in paper and fabric by* KAREN BORLAND.
    (h) BRACELET *in acrylic and paint by* ROWENA PARK.

8 · The Seventies

A new generation was now graduating from the art schools which the revival of the sixties had brought into existence and in the natural course of events the revolutionaries of 1958 became the establishment of 1968. The student sit-ins were the negative manifestation of a new attitude, the positive side of which was a different approach to design. The naturalism of the sixties had sprung quite spontaneously from a concentrated source. The limited art-school set-up of that time meant that ideas were transmitted almost unconsciously, resulting in a single broad stream of invention. Diversity of ideas in 1958 would have meant that the revival would have been still-born, frittered away in a multiplicity of contrasting styles, each with an output too small to overwhelm the indifference of press and public.

By the end of the sixties the situation was reversed: the public was very receptive to new ideas, sometimes, it seemed, at the expense of their critical faculties. Purchase tax eventually disappeared to be replaced by Value Added Tax at what at that time was a more favourable rate, and there was still a reservoir of surplus cash to spend on luxuries. Now there are almost as many styles as there are designers, so original is today's output.

Until the late sixties it could still be said that jewellery techniques had changed little since the Renaissance. Most of the advances made in the nineteenth century were the result not of invention and innovation, but of the rediscovery of very ancient methods—Etruscan granulation and Byzantine plique-à-jour for example. There was some timid use of aluminium but seldom in a way which made the most of its unique qualities. The first half of the twentieth century brought us platinum and investment casting, but from the technical point of view very little else.

As much as anything it had been the relatively high cost of platinum and diamonds which turned the young jeweller of the early sixties towards natural crystals and 18-carat gold. Demand had now made crystals rather expensive: there was something of a fad for them, not only in jewellery but as ornamental nick-nacks. Gold, too had soared in value to a price near that of platinum. But it was not simply economics which prompted the jeweller to seek out new materials. 18-carat gold was closely associated with the free naturalism of the sixties. Silver, which lent itself to the shaping of clearly defined even-textured forms, was a natural alternative. There were still other possibilities less obvious and more challenging: the refractory metal titanium with its extraordinary rainbow patina, glowing acrylics and enamel-like polyesters and, in utter contrast, organic materials like ivory, tortoiseshell, mother-of-pearl and wood.

TITANIUM AND THE REFRACTORY METALS

Although titanium has been exploited in industry since before the First World War, the craftsman has only begun to make use of it in the last ten or twelve years. Titanium must surely be the most cussed and intractable of the jeweller's metals, difficult to bend, emboss or forge, impossible to weld or solder. What it does have to offer the craftsman is a patina so varied and brilliant as to overwhelm all its disadvantages. Heat or a small electrical charge floods the normally silver-grey surface of the metal with iridescent colour, peacock blue, lime green, maroon, amber and every intermediate tint. The patina is caused by a film of oxide which although colourless and transparent in itself causes an interference effect very like that which gives the iridescence to a soap bubble. The thickness of the oxide film increases with the voltage or the temperature and the colour changes accordingly.

Edward de Large (born 1949) studied at Camberwell and the Royal College of Art. He won the Sanderson award and went to Japan to study metal patination and inlay. Trained as a silversmith he was introduced to titanium during his studies.

Electricity gives more accuracy and control over the work than heat and Edward de Large has invented his own techniques and equipment to paint his miniature landscapes. The instrument he has devised is an ordinary paintbrush wired by its metal ferrule to the supply. The bristles have to be wetted, usually with ammonium sulphate solution to transmit the current, and the picture is built up from minute dots. The pictures themselves are disturbing dream landscapes: blinded skyscraper blocks rise from a desert; grave-like rectangular pits yawn in an achingly bare plain beneath a steely sunset. De Large is fascinated by the idea of flight and feels that he is influenced by René Escher. We see many of his landscapes from an airborne vantage point so that the tips of pyramids penetrate a floor of cloud and swimming pools reflect a summer sky. Sometimes flight becomes levitation when huge monoliths float in the chilly air. They are visions of a once-inhabited planet, of life beyond the looking glass, hauntingly vivid and precise. The tablets of titanium are set in plain, wide silver frames as brooches and pendants (Colour Plate XXIb).

Recently an unexpectedly playful element has entered this work. The silver frames are no longer severe and precise but foreshorten and undulate like a flying carpet

136. *Gold, ivory and titanium* COLLAR *by* KAREN LAWRENCE

137. Two ivory, metal and pearl shell BROOCHES *by* KAREN LAWRENCE

whilst within them brilliantly patterned sails, kites and paper darts sway and billow like washing on a line.

De Large also makes torcs and bracelets that are simple, pretty and effective, penannular in design and simply formed from thin titanium rod (Colour Plate XXIc). The haloed spots with which they are sometimes decorated are made simply by introducing a current into drops of water on the surface.

Karen Lawrence (born 1950) works in titanium, although in her hands it seems to shed its overtones of space-age technology and become the fairy metal that its name suggests. She too was a student at Hornsey although she feels that it was not until the end of her time there that her work began to take off. Her work at this time has a strongly Egyptian flavour, the blue of the titanium suggesting the lapis lazuli of pharaonic jewellery (Plate 136). From this time date the 'scarab' rings with their wire-wrapped shoulders.

She moved then to very simple designs: a necklace from this period has the careless delicacy of a daisy chain—dolphin-blue sequins of titanium scattered with ivory florets. A bracelet was of titanium discs overlapping like fish-scales between borders of coiled gold wire.

Around 1977 she started making what she calls her peep-show jewels inspired by the cardboard cut-out entertainments housed in a shoe box that she made as a child (Plate 137). There is something Japanese about these enchanting jewels and her two titanium swans in flight across an ivory moon would not be out of place on a Hokusai print.

Titanium cannot readily be cast or embossed. This is a pity since the shifting iridescence of the oxide film shows at its best on a compound curve. It was partly this which persuaded *Clarissa Mitchell* to conduct her experiments in titanium sputtering while she was studying at the Royal College of Arts. Her objective was to deposit a thin film of titanium on a three-dimensional surface by bombarding it with atoms of the metal. She discovered that a surprising variety of materials could be coated with titanium like this, including marble, silver, porcelain and glass, with effects that depended upon the nature of the underlying surface. Clarissa Mitchell's more orthodox work in the refractory metals is just as striking, brilliantly scaled and plumed collars and bracelets which make the greatest possible use of the metal's properties (Colour Plate XX).

Tantalum and niobium not only colour more brilliantly than titanium, but they can be formed with a hammer, much as silver can, with the extra advantage that they do not harden appreciably whilst they are being worked. Undoubtedly more experimental work remains to be done on the refractory metals in the jewellery workshop.

THE PLASTICS

Plastics have been with us for a long time: celluloid and bakelite were everyday materials well before the First World War and vulcanite, a form of hard rubber, was used as a substitute for jet in cheap mourning jewellery back in the 1860s. The plastics were always an ersatz, an inferior stand-in for something better, bakelite for wood, celluloid for ivory or tortoiseshell, vulcanite for ebony or jet.

After the Second World War the intrinsic qualities of the plastics were at last recognized and they came to be used as an excellent material in their own right, but usually for mass production: industrial art as we called it at the time. In the thirties some cheap plastic costume jewellery was actually carved by hand, much of it in the Jura region of France. It was only in the last decade that the British artist jeweller discovered the unique properties of the plastics—lightness, translucency, colour and tensile strength. Today the jeweller will not hesitate to use acrylic alongside 18-carat gold and will lavish the same time and skill on it as a lapidary might in cutting an emerald.

Roger Morris (born 1940) learned his trade the hard way, but there is a certain inevitability about his progress through business studies and a securely pensioned post in the civil service to his present eminence as one of our most talented jewellers.

The Seventies

His last government job was that of managing a supply depot of artists materials: he began drawing and sketching himself and discovered in this challenges and a sense of elation which he realized his work could never give him. He applied for a place at his local art school and resigned from the civil service as soon as he was accepted. His inclinations at first were towards the fine arts, but at the end of a year, on the advice of his tutors, he opted for three-dimensional design and applied for a place in the jewellery department of the Central School of Arts.

Roger gained much from his three years at the Central and it was here that he first learned the lapidary techniques which were to set him on the path to his own highly individual style. From the Central he went on to a post-graduate course at the Royal College of Art, where he discovered the pantograph machine, using it to cut trailing grooves in agate, often following the course of its natural striations, and inlaying them with gold or silver wires.

Using such an intractable material Roger soon found his creative intellect outstripping his hands. He was fizzing with ideas that he had no time to translate into reality and felt that he had no alternative but to find a softer material which was quicker to work. At this time he was very impressed with the work of the German jewellers like Claus Bury and Fritz Maierhoffer and it was they who introduced him to the acrylic plastics with their easy working consistency and a dazzling palette which graduated from the softest pastels to glaring fluorescents.

Acrylics opened up limitless possibilities although his earlier work in agate was to influence profoundly his handling of this exciting new material: the way in which his acrylics are laminated in subtly related bands of colour must have been prompted by the natural striations in agate. At first the new medium presented him with difficulties in adjustment. His designs called for wafer-thin sheets of plastic of far thinner gauge than any produced commercially. At first he made them with a milling machine, now he finds he gets the same result much more economically with a small circular saw. The soft organic finish or 'feel' of his work is not the result of orthodox polishing: his method is to lap the surface on very fine wet/dry emery paper and then to rub in beeswax. A sort of jigsaw decoration appears in many Roger Morris jewels like a fretted coastline or a cumulus cloud (Colour Plate XXId), together with bold backgrounds of brightly coloured stripes (Colour Plate XXIa). The massive three- or four-sided frames of precious metal which enclose many of his inlays have the dual purpose of containing and emphasizing the design and of protecting the delicate acrylic (Colour Plate XXIe). Sometimes two such elements are connected by a grill of widely spaced vertical bars, a motif which he uses in other contexts.

Like so many of his contemporaries he sees his jewels as miniature sculptures and he has made a series of pyramids, the summits of which are detachable as brooches and often conceal a matching ring. He is sensitive also to the fact that as well as being an aesthetically pleasing object, a jewel is also in a way a toy. Men who buy cats' eyes and alexandrites do so for the simple pleasure they get from watching the stone change with the vagaries of the light. Women turn rings around their fingers or fiddle with beads and pendants, and worry beads and rosaries are made specifically to be manipulated. One of the qualities which the Chinese revere so much in jade is that it is so pleasant to the touch. With this in mind Roger sometimes incorporates into his jewels 'something to fiddle with' — a sapphire stud or a rotating button of plastic. Recently he has been making jewels entirely in contrasting coloured gold.

Susanna Heron's early jewels in silver and polyester resin are well known. A typical necklace would be of three linked oval plaques, each with an oystercatcher flying into it as though trying to get back into the egg. Bird and frame are worked out of silver in a pure silhouette and the spaces filled à jour with red, turquoise and ultramarine resin (Plate 138). Flowers and fishing boats were treated in the same way. In much of this work, however, the frame is quite plain, a simple rim of silver enclosing a membrane of polyester, the colours shifting and blending, congealing into clouds and swirls. The method was to lay the silver frame on a formica surface on which the design was sketched and then to pour the resin in, working the colours together as they set like a water-colourist, sometimes introducing fragments of shattered polyester. This type of pendant or necklace was hung on snake-like Brazilian chain. Bracelets were made in a similar way, two concentric rings of polyester, the intervening space filled with resin. Finger rings with a lunette of polyester arching high above the finger were another development of this. Susanna Heron believes that jewellery should stand clear of the body and yet be an extension of it—like fins on a fish.

Born in Welwyn Garden City in 1949 she spent her childhood in London and Cornwall and became interested in jewellery quite early on. In 1965 she was at Breon O'Casey's evening classes at Redruth School of Art making the kind of things she wanted to wear herself. She took her foundation course at the Falmouth School of Art and went from there to the Central.

A powerful sense of direction guides her work. Each step follows logically from the last, and no matter how far the leap forward it always takes off from a firm springboard. The 1977 Fourways Exhibition which she shared with Caroline Broadhead, Julia Mannheim and Nuala Jamieson was not only a great success, it was a dialogue between the four of them which had a mutual influence on their work.

She had felt for some time that it was taking too long for her to realize her designs and decided to make a change in medium and technique. The first of her perspex jewels was made at this time. The idea was to produce jewels which people could afford. Disarmingly simple they are fretted out of thin sheet and resemble a

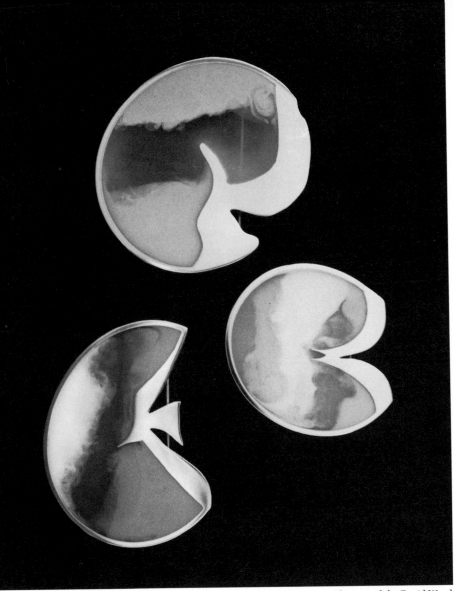

138. Silver and resin
BROOCHES *by*
SUSANNA HERON

Photograph by David Ward

draughtsman's French curve (Plate 139). Four hundred and fifty of the shapes were cut out by an East End sign-maker and finished by hand.

The jubilee neckpieces were made in 1977 for a Victoria and Albert Museum Exhibition, huge annuli of perspex sheet circumscribed with eccentric rings of bright resin. The curves are the most exciting of this series. In spite of the material—very thick perspex—there is something primeval about them: boar's tusk or boomerang, they hang about the neck like a vast question mark (Plate 141). They are sensuously comfortable too, lightly gripping the back of the neck and giving a reassuring nudge to the collarbone. Susanna colours the inner rim of the curves with paint to give a

152

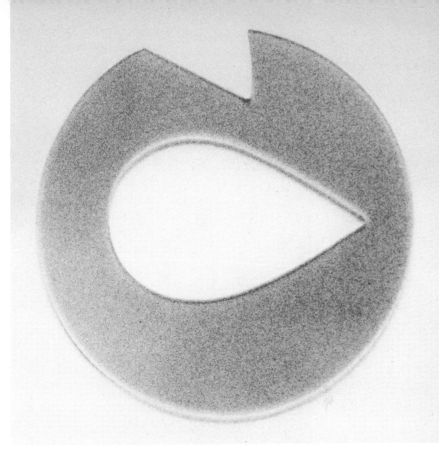

139. Acrylic BRACELETS *by*
SUSANNA HERON

variety of effects: in clear plastic opalescence flows through it, in matt-finished translucent material the colour fades out a little way from the edge like the rind of a melon.

Nuala Jamieson worked in plastics from the beginning. Born in Lisburn, Northern Ireland in 1948 she was trained at the Ulster College of Art and Design and the Central, from which she graduated in 1972. In the same year she participated in the Goldsmiths' Hall graduate training scheme which was concerned mainly with the mass-production side of the jewellery industry. She joined Julia Mannheim (see page 171) and Caroline Broadhead (see page 168) in setting up a workshop in Covent Garden.

Her earliest work used an inlay of simple repeated perspex motifs embedded in polyester resin and framed in silver. Eye-like rings and bold washer-like bangles were decorated in this style, their surfaces lapped to a smooth finish.

While she was at home having a baby in 1975 she worked on textile designs. The rhythmic quality of this work spilled over into her jewels resulting in a series of designs in which a repeated pattern is drilled or incised into clear plastic and the recesses then filled with polyester resin similarly to champlevé enamel.

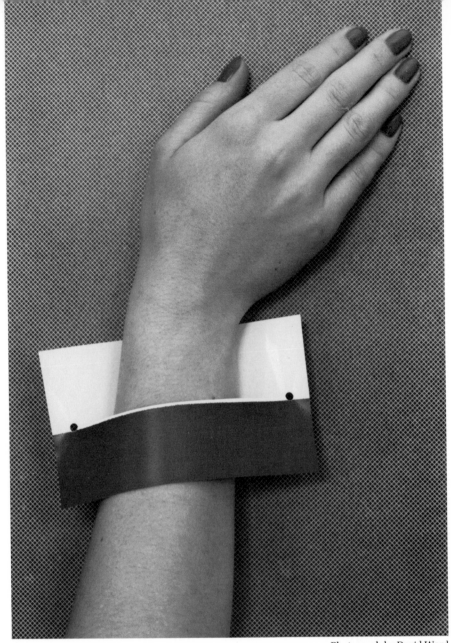

Photograph by David Ward

140. PVC BRACELET *by* SUSANNA HERON

Nuala began experimenting with textile dyes on plastic in 1976. First in the new series of jewels which resulted from this were perspex bracelets fluted like a piecrust and tinted with multi-coloured dyes. Heat was needed to help the dye to penetrate; at first she used a kiln but found later that sparing use of the flame was the best method (Colour Plate XXIIa,b,c and f).

Photograph by David Ward

141. Perspex COLLAR *by* SUSANNA HERON

JEWELS AND SCULPTURE

Change in the seventies went far deeper than material and technique. All the previous ideas about what jewellery is and should be were pulled apart and re-examined. A sculptor's eye was mercilessly brought to bear upon jewellery design whose objective till then had been simply to please a woman. The traditional idea that a jewel should fit snugly to a woman's body and personality and add lustre to both was no longer enough. Two new ideas grew up, apparently opposite and yet both springing from the same attitude of mind. Firstly that a jewel could be a significant work of art in isolation from its owner, secondly that the wearer should react with a jewel to form a sculptural whole with it.

David Watkins (born 1940) makes jewels which both look and feel extraordinary. His very large structures of glowing translucent acrylic are designed for the special occasion and only a few women have the presence and unashamed nerve to wear them. He was trained as a sculptor and his great preoccupation is with the relationships of structures to people. A woman is meant to feel his jewels and be aware of them: to wear them is a contrived and conscious act just as singing is

155

compared to speech or dancing to walking. Watkins knows that they are physically inhibiting, the intention is that they should be psychologically liberating.

Some of his designs depend upon movement, particularly those bracelets made with two gimballed hoops, one pivoted within the other. Conversely many pieces are designed for their rigidity because, as he says, of 'the way they section the body mass'.

Much of his work is in acrylic rod sand-blasted to a matt finish and heightened with slim transverse bands of 18-carat gold. Clasps and fittings are always perfectly simple, but efficient and reliable and beautifully engineered (Colour Plate XXIIId). His aim is for the perfect piece and he will go to great lengths to approach as closely as possible to his ideal.

About a third of Watkins's work is commissioned and many of his clients seem to be Americans, probably, he thinks, because they have the self-assurance to wear his jewels.

David Watkins shares a workshop with his wife *Wendy Ramshaw* (born 1939) but although they have certain attitudes in common their relationship is the very antithesis of the Arts and Crafts working partnership. Their jewels remain obstinately dissimilar, the result of a self-conscious effort to preserve their own individuality. Although one of them may see the other embarking on a work which seems on the face of it preposterous and destined to failure, he or she will bite their tongue and be surprised to see it come out right in the end. In the course of a busy day neither finds the time for mutual criticism, but beneath their almost ferocious independence one senses that this is a relationship that stimulates, provokes and catalyses: it is impossible not to speculate upon the paths they might have taken if they had not met.

Wendy is best known for her rings, fantastical structures impossible to ignore, either by watcher or wearer. The earliest were massive, their towering bezels elaborately turned on the lathe into bobbin-like forms and ringed with bands of enamel. Best known though are her multiple rings—groups of rings in gold, silver and semi-precious stones, designed to be worn all at once in an endless variety of combinations and even to be slipped over a little tower of perspex or bronze when they are not in wear as a miniature sculpture (Colour Plate XXIIIa, b and c). Once she tried the exercise of feeding one of her designs into a computer to find out how many changes could be rung on it: the permutations ran into millions.

She also conceived the idea of relating her designs to a rectangular frame. Sometimes irrepressibly squiggling calligraphic motifs are sandwiched between two abacus-like frames in sand-blasted gold, whereas another closely related family of designs depends on strong verticals contrasted with horizontal squiggles in a way which suggests musical notation or the stops and valves on a trumpet.

Meanwhile the ring designs have undergone continual change and development and now the slender multiple shanks sprout spires, darts and arrowheads. They are both savage and sophisticated like the emblems of a fierce and ancient priesthood. In a way this is deliberate: she knows quite well than an unplanned movement will snare a garment or upset a glass, but she feels that this self-awareness will invest simple movements with a ceremonial quality. Her jewels, like those of her husband, seem to be created for the modern party at which nobody dances but which is in itself a kind of ritual dance. They are the regalia of an impromptu ceremony with its own peculiar genuflexions and incantations at which what you say seems to be less important than the way you say it.

Pierre Degen's concern is with what his jewels do to the surface they are worn on and the shadows they cast, and the tucks, plucks and gathers they make in a garment are obviously more important to him than the ornaments themselves. Born in 1947, he was trained in Switzerland. He now works at Hornsey as a part-time lecturer, and this arrangement is what keeps him in London, since nowhere else could he earn a living and pursue his own experiments at the same time. In a sense his jewels are as insubstantial as the images cast by a slide projector and to create them he uses whatever comes to hand: brightly coloured polythene tubing, scraps of nylon mesh, plastic toy figures—it does not matter what they are for, here the shadow is more important than the substance.

Pierre Degen shares the contemporary fascination with kites and early aeroplanes, and the thrumming tightly stretched webs and filaments of their structure are an important feature of his work.

Pierre is using fine-bore nickel tubing and springy watch pivot-wire strung together and tensioned with the silk thread used to bind fishing rods. These pieces are light and skeletal, depending for their effect upon the shadows they cast on the wearer's body, doubling, fading, lengthening and foreshortening with every movement relative to the source of light (Plate 142).

SCIENCE FICTION AND SPACE AGE TECHNOLOGY

The work of many of these craftsmen seems to group itself quite naturally into a distinct school which originated in the early seventies and which continues to evolve and develop. To call it mechanistic is not only an oversimplification, it is wildly inaccurate, for these designs are both romantic and fantastic. Asimov and Ballard are the literary cousins of Watkins and Pierre Degen just as Geddes and Barrie were the artistic kin of Mackintosh and the Macdonald sisters.

Joel Degen (born 1941) is not related to Pierre; and the difference in their respective approaches is quite fundamental so there is no possibility of their being confused

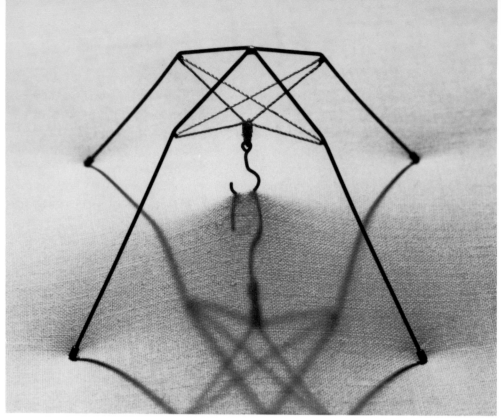

142. A 'BROOCH' in steel pivot wire and silk thread by PIERRE DEGEN

(Plates 143, 144). Joel Degen has carried his involvement with modern technology so far as to make use of its artifacts in his jewels. There is something gem-like about the electronic paraphernalia of bulbs, fuses, resistances and the like, tiny ampoules of glass protecting minute whiskers of metal as though they were holy relics, and Joel Degen organizes them cleverly into brooches and pendants with accuracy and a keen sense of balance. His rings are set with aircraft nosewheels or deeply scored with cooling fins, or riveted together like an engine component (Colour Plate XIX).

Eric Spiller's (born 1946) designs hint at the awful mysteries of space-age technology. They engage attention and arouse curiosity: bangles of multicoloured discs neatly bolted between hoops of bright metal (Plate 145) and exquisitely colour-keyed ring brooches. Do they come from the appalling white-hot guts of the atomic reactor or are they a small but vital part of a space satellite? Whatever the answer, the care and accuracy with which these little jewels are made makes them both pleasing and precious.

Courtesy of the Worshipful Company of Goldsmiths

143. Silver RINGS *by* JOEL DEGEN

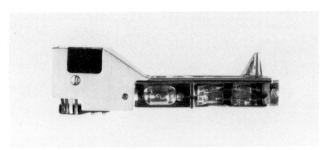

Courtesy of the Worshipful Company of Goldsmiths

144. A silver BROOCH *by* JOEL DEGEN

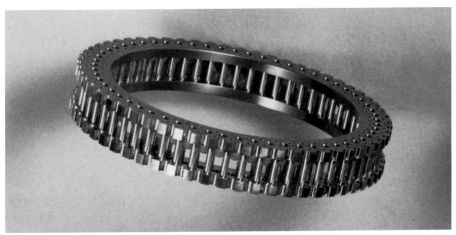

Courtesy of the Worshipful Company of Goldsmiths

145. A BRACELET *by* ERIC SPILLER

NOSTALGIA

Like our mid-Victorian ancestors we live in an age of breakneck social and technological change and we sometimes protect ourselves from it just as they did by looking back into the past. Some jewels, particularly the fine inlaid work of *Rosamund Conway* (born 1951) and *Beverley Phillips*, recall the geometrical style of the twenties although this was as much a natural development as a conscious effort at imitation and revival (Plate 146). In *Deborah Cowin's* earrings we can see the clean line and no-nonsense simplicity of the Bauhaus (Colour Plate XXVIIb). But it seemed as though in the nineteen-seventies we were more in pursuit of a personal rather than a histori-

Courtesy of the Worshipful Company of Goldsmiths

146. Two BROOCHES *of inlaid wood, shell and ivory by* BEVERLEY PHILLIPS

cal past. The most powerful urge was to recreate the sights, scenes and memories of an ideal childhood and it manifested itself in different ways.

Barbara Cartlidge (born 1922) frankly describes her jewels as toys: bracelets are mounted with roundabouts and scenic railways (Plate 147), and in her puppet-show pendant, Mr Punch and the policeman can actually be made to move. She loved dolls' houses as a child and each of the silver doors so cleverly hinged into her jewels conceals a domestic Lilliput of bedrooms, bathrooms and kitchen, complete to the minutest detail.

Gunilla Treen's (born 1949) jewels call to mind those puzzles to be found in Christmas crackers; glass-topped boxes with ball-bearings which have to be coaxed into a clown's eyes or through a maze. Her compartmented boxes are sawn out of opaque acrylic which is then sandwiched between two clear layers and pinned

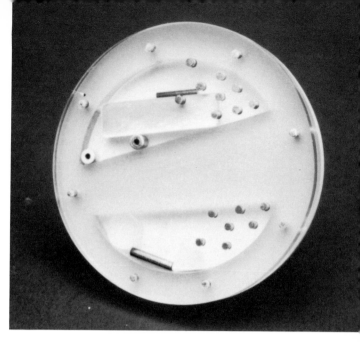

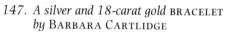

147. A silver and 18-carat gold BRACELET *by* BARBARA CARTLIDGE

148. An acrylic 'puzzle' BROOCH *by* GUNILLA TREEN *(enlarged)*

together (Plate 148). The compartments enclose an assortment of free-rolling objects like cubes or discs of malachite, lapis lazuli or mother-of-pearl, or small glass beads, an interesting alternative to traditional setting techniques which allows the gems to settle in various patterns like a kaleidoscope.

The earlier jewels of *Marlene McKibbins* would not look out of place dangling from the hood of a pram with their frank cheerful colours and guileless basic shapes. A necklace was strung from perspex cylinders and discs of red, green and yellow felt. Another was of clear polythene tubing superimposed with acetate rosettes like children's toy windmills.

Alexandra Anne Dick (born 1951) takes her ideas from the fauna and flora of childhood (Plate 149). The beautiful conkers she made were designed to be hung round the neck by their strings. The most realistic were of figured yew wood, the floury indentation represented by an inlay of ivory or silver—these presented problems because the wood with the finest grain was very prone to cracking. Others were of stainless steel inlaid with gold, the schoolboy's dream of an ultimate and indestructible super-conker.

Lexi Dick makes gloriously funny fish, not lithe and dart-like but appealingly chubby—fish a child could easily catch in a sixpenny net. They gambol as cufflinks or meet and kiss as a pendant.

One style in particular invaded large areas of the decorative and graphic arts. Trees and clouds are the dominant forms, very two-dimensional, depicted in masses of flat unshaded tone with simple billowing outlines. One thinks of children's book

161

149. A silver, slate and crystal tadpole NECKLACE *by* LEXI DICK

illustrations of the early thirties, of cartoon films, particularly *Yellow Submarine*, or perhaps of the world as we might see it under the influence of a hallucinatory drug. A great deal of *Catherine Mannheim*'s (born 1943) work is in this style (Plate 150), but with slightly sinister overtones which suggest Magritte—a landscape of storm-clouds glimpsed through a window for example. *Ellen Chapman*'s (born 1950) superb head-dress is a close-fitting helmet of massed clouds pierced to show a fractured rainbow of azure and copper-red enamels scattered with sapphires (Plate 151).

162

150. *Jewels by* CATHERINE MANNHEIM

　(a) PENDANT *in silver, 18-carat gold and spray paint*

　(b) *A grid* BROOCH *in chrysoprase, silver and 18-carat gold*

　(c) *A rainbow* BROOCH *in silver, 18-carat gold, awabe shell and spray paint*

　(d) *A cloud and palm-tree* BROOCH *in silver, titanium and 18-carat gold*

　(e) *A window* BROOCH *in silver, 18-carat gold and titanium*

　(f) *Silver and 18-carat gold* RINGS

151. A HEAD-DRESS *by* ELLEN CHAPMAN *(reduced)*

SURREALISM

There is a powerful element of fantasy in many modern jewels as though they had been created to give us insights into other worlds, alternative realities which exist no more than a dream's breadth away. We sense it in the work of Catherine Mannheim and we see it in Edward de Large's titanium dreamscapes. The little shrouded figures that appear in some of Pierre Degen's constructions are pregnant with passive menace, and David Hensel's voluptuous serpent-bodied mer-women seem to have been created to navigate the dark tides of our personal nightmares.

At his degree show, *Douglas Wagstaffe* showed a group of pendants, each of which was about as pretty as any army field-compass. It was almost as though Wagstaffe was striving after ugliness as a kind of ideal. The jewels were put together with nuts and bolts: one was set with an amber-glass teddy bear's eye in a mink-fur surround; another gimballed like a microscope mirror with a leggy insect silhouetted on a prismatic ground like a fly's eye; in a third the fur of some wretched small mammal bristles over draculine false fangs. Unfortunately Wagstaffe now seems to have abandoned jewellery for silversmithing.

Mitchell Nugent is an American who has been living and working in South Wales since 1972. There is a teasing sense of mischief about his witty jewels (Plate 152). He

152. Gold and fire-opal PENDANT *and* EARRINGS *by* MITCHELL NUGENT

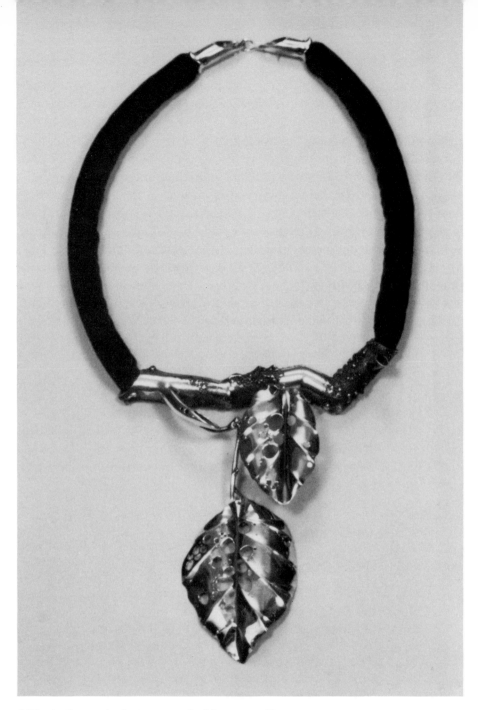

153. *A silver and velvet* COLLAR *by* MITCHELL NUGENT

takes the more threadbare clichés of the art nouveau revival, turns them upside-down and shakes them into disconcerting life. The dragonfly on his pendant has the face of a saucy imp; his mermaid is a gorgeous big-breasted negress who croons a submarine melody in a flood of golden bubbles. His apple leaves are devoured by insects, scabbed and blighted with rusty-red patina; they hang, not from a chain but from a thick roll of blousy velvet (Plate 153).

Stephen Bort (born 1955) is a great admirer of David Hockney. He is also very sympathetic to German ideas of what a jewel should be and sees no reason why its owner should not display it as a piece of sculpture if he wants to. Games motifs are prominent in his earlier work and he admits to being delighted when an old lady at his degree show asked 'are they little games'. Bald and beautiful phrenologists' heads and wellington-booted feet appear often in his jewels, most of which are brooches, cryptic miniature tableaux encased in aquaria of clear acrylic. Bort interprets his designs with skill making clever use of inlaid lapis lazuli and studs of gold sunk flush into silver.

NATURE AND THE NATURAL MATERIALS

Diverse although the output of the jeweller was in the first half of the seventies it seemed to be moving in two distinct and opposite directions; on the one hand back into the misty and not always reassuring world of dreams and childhood; on the other into the gleaming and terrifyingly efficient future.

By this time, of course, we had begun to think very seriously about the environment, about our polluted towns and poisoned and dwindling countryside, begun to doubt the real effectiveness of the technological society. The energy crisis made these questions even more relevant. The British turn instinctively to the land in times of trouble, for the idea of 'three acres and a cow' lies buried deep in our national psyche. As the trim back lawns were replaced by cabbages and leeks, natural motifs began to appear more and more in jewellery and the craftsman turned to materials which had simply grown rather than been processed or synthesized.

Mathew Tomalin (born 1945) makes his jewels of wood: russet yew, silvery ash, pale box, in a way which pays tribute to the trees they come from. A slice of finely figured yew bearing three golden fruit is set on an ivory trunk; the open centre of an oval pendant of grey ash is hung with a trembling leaf of mother-of-pearl; a thick tube of yew forms a ring, the upper surface wrinkled with the fine fluting one sees on barked timber.

David Courts and *Bill Hackett* strip nature down to its bare anatomy in beautifully

The Seventies

sculpted and articulated jewels which represent the skeleton of a snake, a fish or a frog (Plate 154).

John Fenn sets his work with plaques of engraved glass: a pendant engraved with meadow flowers is surmounted by a cast-silver grasshopper which looks as though it might spring away at the touch of a finger.

Nature triumphs again in *Pamela Dickson*'s work. Round turquoises pop out of the front of a bracelet like peas from a pod, garnets ooze from a gold ring like juice from a bruised fruit. *David Ian Doxford* accurately reproduces small, natural, found objects like nasturtium seeds, ash keys, limpets and ammonites in gold. *Michael Burton* (born 1949) takes his inspiration from the village rather than the hedgerow or the shore and his ivory or boxwood rings are carved with a cottage or a church (Plate 155).

In contrast, *Caroline Broadhead*'s (born 1950) treatment of ivory was extremely sophisticated, deceiving the eye into thinking that this tough material can in some way be made as malleable as butter or as flexible as a piece of string (Plate 156). Ivory

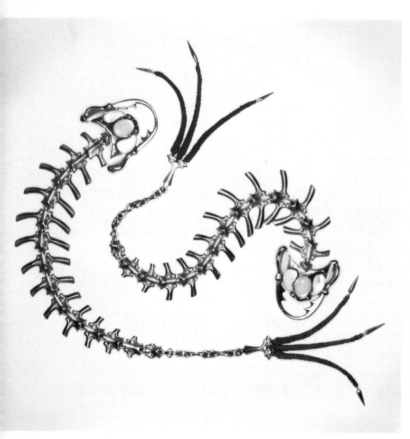

154. *18-carat gold, opal and silk* BRACELETS *by* COURTS *and* HACKETT *(reduced)*

155. RINGS *in boxwood and ivory by* MICHAEL BURTON

Courtesy of the Worshipful Company of Goldsmiths

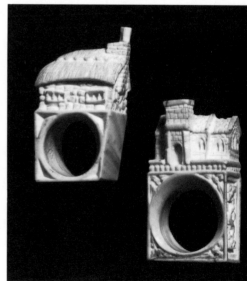

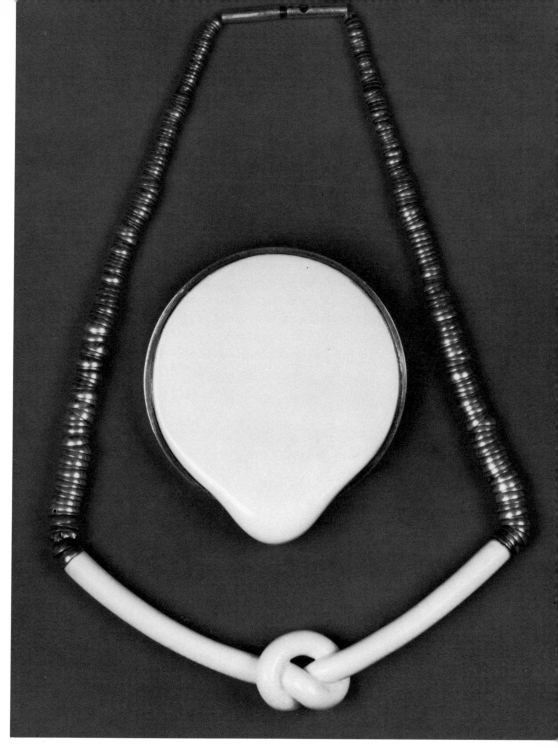

156. A BROOCH *and a* NECKLACE *in silver and ivory by* CAROLINE BROADHEAD

erupts from the bezel of a ring like a fountain of shaving cream, contorts into an overhand knot or melts and drips like candlewax at the front of a necklace; earstuds look like dollops of whipped cream. There is a topsy-turvy sense of fun in these jewels and, as in all of her work, more than meets the eye at first glance.

Ivory fascinated her: its grain and texture varied not only from region to region, but also from animal to animal. She became more and more saddened and worried by the fate of the elephant and her anxiety was confirmed on a trip by road from Tunisia to Kenya. But there was no substitute for ivory: nothing, it seemed could match its soft translucency and delicate grain. Characteristically she solved the problem by taking a completely different direction. The brush jewels were the result: hooped wooden girdles, bracelets and collars gorgeously tufted with nylon monofilament like the finery of some Amazonian chief (Colour Plate XXIId). Three or four years ago she started working in cotton, the fibres teased into great moplike agglomerations with the same spirit of gaiety which she brings to all her work.

David Hensel (born 1945) has always worked in the organic materials. He began by studying medicine and the natural sciences but with his kind of innate skill it was

Courtesy of the Worshipful Company of Goldsmiths

157 (a) and (b). A pomander RING *by* DAVID HENSEL *representing the members of his family carved and inlaid in wood, ivory, mother-of-pearl and silver, open and closed*

158. A bracelet *by* Julia Mannheim *in silver and mother-of-pearl*

inevitable that he should gravitate towards the arts and he finished his education at Brighton College of Arts.

His work embodies no conscious symbolism, corresponds to no private mythology, but its emotional content is very important to him (Plate 157). Carved by him in ivory, a young circus-girl contortionist arches around the wrist as a bracelet. She clasps a cockatoo to her breast, its feathers are dusted with gold, her meagre costume spangled with opals. It is grotesque, but touched with poetry and pathos. An African blackwood fish, beaked and crescent-tailed also makes a bangle, its lithe body crusted with silver—not, it appears, netted from some bottomless pool at full moon but, according to the craftsman, borrowed from the illustrations in a book on tropical fish. The bubbling silvery encrustation on this and on other pieces of his is obtained by electroforming directly on to the wood (Colour Plate XXVd and e).

Julia Mannheim's (born 1949) earlier work was in silver and champlevé enamel but after a while she found enamelling myopic and inhibiting: instead of expanding her creative horizons she felt that her work was beginning to grow in upon itself.

Her discovery of ebony and mother-of-pearl resulted inevitably in a complete change in design and technique. The new designs were very simple on the face of it, bracelets of plain polished ebony ferruled and socketed with silver which please the hand as well as the eye.

For a while she worked with Nuala Jamieson and Caroline Broadhead in their

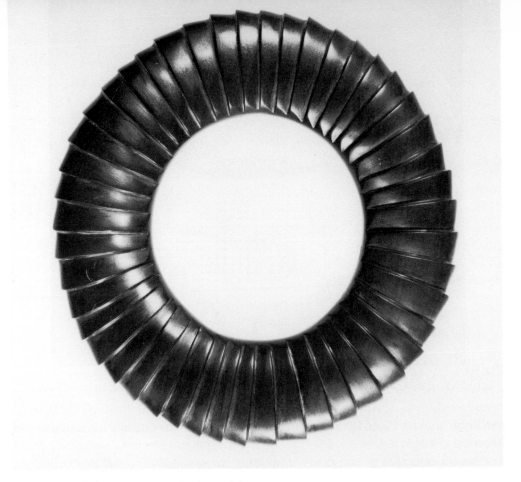

159. *A carved ebony* BRACELET *by* JULIA MANNHEIM

160. *Carved boxwood and beech* RING *and* HAT BROOCH *by* JULIA MANNHEIM

Covent Garden workshop and joined them in the Fourways Exhibition (see page 153). Julia knows her materials and how to make the most of them. One of her designs adapts as readily to a ring as a bracelet: a short tube of silver encompassed by a circlet of cleft wood or shell, fat and thin in places, slanting and undulating, contrasting the wildness of the native material with the cool perfection of the silver (Plate 158).

The most interesting of her bracelets have no metal on them at all. Although abstract in design they convey a great range of mood from the homely to the almost sinister, whether goffered like a piecrust or scaled like an armadillo (Plate 159). The thin rings in blonde boxwood have a dry delicacy like vellum or pressed leaves (Plate 160). Her hat brooches are exuberantly peaked, pleated and crested like old-fashioned millinery (Plate 160).

MYTHOLOGY

This new sensitivity to nature and the rediscovery of organic materials seem to have awakened the craftsman to those primitive, archetypal images which haunt the lower reaches of our consciousness. Myth and magic begin to steal back into jewellery, and the fact that the jeweller invents the fairy-tale herself makes no difference, for the cast, the scenery and the stage-props remain the same: the same castles and sorcerers, golden apples and silver doves.

The extraordinary jewels of *Kevin Coates* (born 1950) are the record of a personal mythology which is philosophical as much as literary. He feels attracted to writers like Macdonald and Hesse and likes children's books too, as much for illustrations by artists like Dulac and Nielson as for the stories themselves. In fact he believes that the illustrator's task is similar to the jeweller's—that of organizing an idea into a limited space.

Coates originally intended to become a musician and studied the violin while he was living with his parents in Australia. Music still plays an important part in his life: he plays professionally the viola d'amore, the lute, the baroque violin and the baroque mandolin which he was responsible for reviving himself. In 1980 he was awarded a doctorate for his thesis on 'The Sacred Geometry in the Design of Renaissance and Baroque Stringed Instruments'.

He is obsessed by the platonic solids and polyhedra and uses them to frame and contain his jewels. One such design is composed with a magpie, a dodecahedron and a distorting mirror, and the geometry of the dodecahedron is explained with engravings on the reverse. In 1974 he was so haunted by news of the deaths of children all over the world that he produced a work with a group of seven children clustered around an ascending flight of white doves; the number seven was dominant in this work even to the number of gold studs inlaid in the titanium.

He uses titanium in most of his jewels and handles this difficult metal with unrivalled virtuosity, devising his own method of joining it and laboriously filing up his minutely detailed figures from the solid.

Dr Coates produces reams of drawings and sketches for each piece before he sits down at the bench. He works mainly on commission and produces about four major pieces a year. As time goes on his work becomes more and more intellectually complex as though he were striving not only for technical perfection but for some

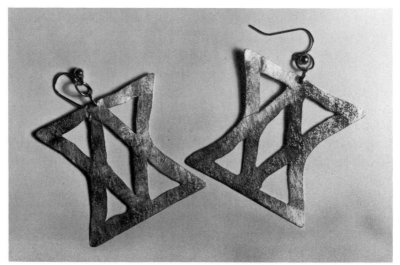

Courtesy of the Worshipful Company of Goldsmiths

161. EARRINGS *by* BREON O'CASEY

personal spiritual goal. His jewels have become icons, objects of contemplation, images on the retina of the mind's eye (Colour Plate XXIV).

Each of *Paul Preston*'s (born 1943) most recent jewels opens a peephole into that parallel world which we commute into so readily as children, but which becomes obscure and inaccessible as we grow older. 'Magus' is a pendant which frames the image of the wild-haired master magician, his ruby eyes aglint. Above him is a bird and over that a sun and a moon. Flames sizzle from the emerald and the water opal which join the Magus jewel to its chain of checkered links. Preston works in 18-carat gold and what looks like oxidized silver but which is in reality white gold clouded by the flame of the blowtorch. His jewels bear inscriptions stamped into the metal itself or tagged on with a little label which tell something of where and when the jewel was made and perhaps give a hint as to what it is about. They have a fine well-weathered look as though their edges have been smoothed off with a thousand years or so of wear, and this makes them very touchable (Colour Plate XXVa, b and c).

One often senses this quality in a modern jewel, as though it originated in some culture distant in both time and space (Colour Plate XXVII). *Breon O'Casey*'s (born 1928) jewels have the sympathetic rough-hammered surfaces one sees in pre-Columbian work (Plate 161). The motifs he uses are the oldest in the world, Maltese crosses, ancient emblem of the sun, flowers and silver moon-pendants all simply cut out of sheet as the ancient Peruvians and Minoans once did. He strings necklaces and bracelets out of pierced pebbles and drum-shaped fish-vertebrae beads that are as old in conception as the craft of metalworking itself.

FERROUS METAL AND CERAMIC

Endlessly inventive and inquisitive, the craftsman now seems ready to make jewellery out of anything, even the cheapest and most commonplace of materials. There is nothing new about iron and steel jewels, however: Benvenuto Cellini mentions the steel rings made in his day and cut steel and Berlin iron were not in the least unusual in the last century.

David Poston (born 1948) makes simple ferrous jewels of exquisite precision: some are perfectly tapered rings of steel for the neck and wrist, others seem as though they might have been suggested by the thimbles, shackles and chandlery used in rigging a sailing craft. *Martha Gumn*'s (born 1955) jewels have a kindliness of texture that one does not expect from such an uncompromisingly masculine metal. She inlays her steel with other metals, diagonal bands of silver on a plain hoop bracelet, concentric rings of gold on a pair of disc-shaped earrings.

Quite recently David Watkins (see page 155) has been working in mild steel. The simplest of these jewels are torcs, the black, hammered steel crimped in a W formation by way of decoration. In complete contrast are those jewels in blued steel progressively graduated in colour and combined with white and yellow gold, and although apparently simple this work makes great demands on the artist's time and skill. Others are of slim wire, disturbingly geometrical and asymmetrical, coated with neoprene which seems to glow although it is not at all luminous.

When *Aileen Hamilton* went from Epsom to the Royal College of Art she discovered in herself a natural instinct for colour. Her previous work in bamboo, tortoiseshell, ivory and ebony suddenly seemed overwhelmingly brown and she felt drawn towards the clean white and translucent colours of ceramic. It was Sandra Eastwood who introduced her to bone china and she soon developed her own methods of making this pure, even-grained material into jewellery.

The Seventies

The clay was cast into wafer-thin geometric shapes and then partially fired. The latticed design was then masked out with thin strips of adhesive tape and the exposed material sand-blasted away. The lace-like forms were then glazed and the enamel colours sprayed on and fired. These cats' cradles and spiderwebs of softly shaded colour are worn knotted on silk cords as necklaces (Colour Plate XXVI).

Wendy Ramshaw (see page 156) now works in porcelain, the fine unglazed paste faintly tinged with an oxide pigment. Those she made while in Australia are explicitly organic: googly-eyed witchity grubs and curious mollusc-like creatures fossilized in even-textured ceramic. The ceramic jewels which she has made since her return have tended more towards the abstract.

TRADITIONAL METHODS AND MATERIALS

In the midst of all this theorizing and experimentation it is interesting that so much of the finest and perhaps the most enduring work of the decade was made by traditional methods in conventional materials. These jewels are no less exciting and original for all that and will probably exist to delight our grandchildren when more arcane designs in less durable modern materials have either worn out or ceased to please.

Jaqueline Mina (born 1942) comes from a musical family: a career as a mezzo-soprano was originally planned for her but it was probably inevitable that she should move towards the visual arts. Hornsey could offer no jewellery course at that time so she chose silversmithing. She finished her training at the Royal College of Art, working for John Donald (see page 123) in the holidays.

Her early work as one might expect at this time was strongly textural, much of it set with uncut stones and crystals. Then she had the chance of seeing and actually handling a collection of ancient Greek jewels and it was this, she feels, that completely changed her approach. There can be no doubt though that she has been profoundly influenced by Sah Oved (see page 85) in the way in which she handles gold.

Jacqueline Mina understands her metal, letting it speak for itself, without burnishing away its warmth or shutting it up in hard outlines. She likes to terminate a line or outline a shape with a playful wiggle and will always avoid filing away a blob of unwanted solder because she believes it changes the character of a piece. She prefers cuttlefish to investment casting and makes the most of its natural grain.

A major piece like 'Ecstasy' is the culmination of a painstaking design process, an elaborate succession of models, photographs and sketches. The hardstone carvings are made in Germany and she sends the lapidary a fired porcelain prototype to make sure he gives her what she wants. This is a costly business but she feels that if she were to take this on herself it could only be at the expense of other aspects of her work (Plate 162).

Quite often, however, she works from one rough sketch or even dispenses with a sketch altogether and just snips a jewel out of sheet gold, extemporizing as she goes along. If it does not come off she recycles the pieces for casting. The range of her work is considerable, from curious loofah-like chains of 18-carat gold wire knitted on a bobbin, in the same way that children braid coloured wool, to rings, with an arch of trochus shell shimmering over a froth of gold granulation.

Natural, and especially marine motifs and allusions, are everywhere in her jewels and the Mediterranean influence in them is strongly apparent.

Charlotte de Syllas (born 1946) inhabits her own world, even her own time-scale, pursuing her objectives with a dedication and self-denial which verges on the bloody minded. At seventeen she went to Paris to decide whether to study mime or jewellery and between 1963 and 1966 she was at Hornsey where she came under the wholly benevolent influence of Gerda Flockinger (see page 125).

Out of art school in the late sixties, she began working in steel and it is typical of her that she went straight to the gunsmiths at Purdey's to ask them how to go about blueing steel and inlaying it with gold. When she has a problem she never hesitates to ask the man who knows, but on the other hand she is very generous when it comes to revealing her own working methods.

Her search for exactly the right materials is just as painstaking. She decided to make a silver torc for Gerda Flockinger by the old-fashioned method of cuttlefish casting. The idea was to make it in two parts, and she scoured London suppliers for four pieces of monster cuttlefish big enough for the job. Before pouring the metal she brushed the dust out of the cuttlefish to bare the grain and make a decorative feature of it. The terminals were to be of amber so she went to a big amber dealer for help. They advised her to use perspex, but she was not to be put off; eventually she found what she wanted and is now delighted to see that the amber has worn to a rich dark patina.

She has a deep understanding of the nature and essence of her materials. Iolite has the most spectacular dichroism of any gemstone, sapphire blue from one direction and pale yellow from another. Commissioned to make a collar of these curious gems she cut and pieced them together so that the yellow and blue transparencies were organized into a dramatic pattern. The gems were then set on a band of blued-steel chain-mail splashed with a single asymmetrical blotch of gold.

Every one of her major jewels breaks new ground, obliges her to seek out special materials and learn new techniques. It is planned like a military operation with every stage meticulously plotted, every contingency allowed for, every difficulty anticipated. There is no need for notes or drawings because she has turned the whole

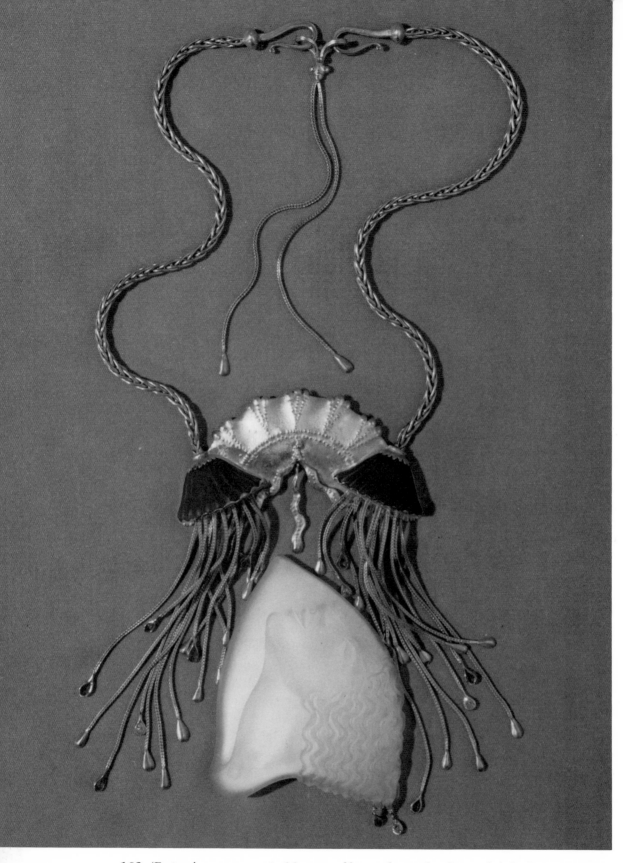

162. 'Ecstasy', a NECKLACE in 18-carat gold, carved crystal and stained chalcedony, emeralds and diamonds by JACQUELINE MINA

thing over and over in her mind until she knows every step by heart and can recall a perfect eidetic image of the finished jewel which is true to a millimetre. A piece like this can be years in the making.

Her jewels contain surprises, sometimes little ones, sometimes throw-away gestures of a prodigality which would be casual if they did not involve so much time and skill. The long fluted steel earrings, for example, which are more richly inlaid on the back than on the front, a crystal face peering from a niche on the reverse of an opal and nephrite Janus-head collar (Colour Plate XXVIII).

She can exploit the sort of quirk or accident that a lesser talent might regard as a misfortune: traces of ash left in the mould of a pair of gold seashell earrings left holes in the finished casting; it would have been a simple matter to fill them, but typically she decided to leave them as they were in a lacy à jour effect.

Jewels need to be cosseted and cherished, hidden from the casual eye like a rare text in a fine binding and her boxes are designed and their materials selected and fashioned with as much care as goes into the setting itself. For example, a ring set with a serene head of carved chalcedony is slotted into a box of superbly grained partridge wood encrusted with fissured gold leaf.

Her work leaves her with no time for theorizing about the role and function of the jeweller. She has said though that she will write a book 'when she is eighty'. If she does it will be a precious contribution to the traditions which she serves with such fierce and unselfconscious devotion.

Like many of her contemporaries in the early seventies *Rosamund Conway* (born 1951) worked in the organic materials. This early work which she did while a student at the Central is abstract and mathematical in conception: lunettes, angles and quadrants in finely inlaid ivory, gold, ebony and tortoiseshell (Plate 163).

In 1973 at the Royal College of Art her style changed abruptly and it was replaced by bulging tarpaulins hitched with straining ropes. She feels, somewhat ruefully, that she has become identified with this phase of her work. It was a time, of course, when the arts were packaging themselves at the drop of a hat, when a whole tract of rockbound Australian coastline was swathed in polythene just to see what it looked like.

She completed the Royal College course in two years instead of three and won a travelling scholarship to Japan. Inevitably she was fascinated by Japanese metalwork, the apparent simplicity which conceals great technical complexity, the inlays which are so spontaneous that they seem to have been applied with a flick of a brush when they are in fact the result of hours and hours of minute and painstaking craftsmanship. It is this work in contrasting precious metals that she has developed with such extraordinary sensitivity in her own jewellery. Yet this is not inlay work in the accepted sense; the technique is her own. Working from careful drawings, the

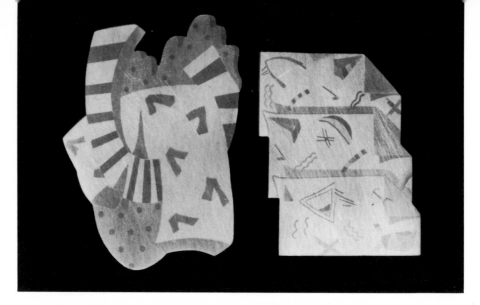

163. Inlaid gold and silver BROOCHES *by* ROSAMUND CONWAY

different elements in the design are sawn out and fitted together edge to edge rather like a jigsaw puzzle and then hard-soldered.

The surfaces which she decorates like this often bulge enticingly like a well-stuffed cushion. Some resemble kites or sails with the tips of the spars just visible. This convexity creates problems, as joints tend to split in the doming process and have to be resoldered, but the result is stronger in consequence. She often makes her own alloys, mixing the different coloured golds as a painter mixes his paints. Colour is the key to her work, but she dislikes precious stones.

Leo de Vroomen was born in 1941 in the Netherlands; he went to work in Switzerland after serving the Dutch four-year apprenticeship. He first came to Britain to learn English, dividing his time between working for David Thomas (see page 120) and teaching at the Central. Eventually he set up his own workshop. He has always been a great admirer of early Dutch silversmithing, particularly the 'auricular' repoussé work of Adam van Vianen—until he learned how to do it himself, he found it hard to believe that such extraordinarily convoluted designs could have been made out of a single sheet of metal. He now works mainly in gold, never making more than a few copies of any design and then only by hand methods (Plate 164). *Ginny de Vroomen* (born 1947) was trained at Kingston College of Art and London University. She was teaching art metalwork when she met and married Leo in 1970. Nowadays the two work in partnership, with Ginny producing most of the designs.

Leo believes that there is a prevalence of boring designs in the trade because the art schools have so little influence on it. The trade is so firmly convinced that the new designs will not sell that it will not give them the chance. The graduates are just as much to blame, he thinks, because they lack the determination to elbow themselves in with fresh ideas: 'They expect everything to be done for them', he says.

EPHEMERA

In Edwardian times most cheap jewellery simply mimicked the ornaments worn by those higher up the social scale. There were interesting exceptions of course but even the costume jewellery of the nineteen-fifties and sixties although larger and more extravagant than life still flashed and glittered something like the real thing—and was so cheap that it could be worn for a season and then relegated to the back of a drawer.

In the seventies although 'imitation jewellery' continued to be made, cheap jewellery began to take on a character of its own, even to make little visual wisecracks. Like the realistic plastic apple-core pendants they only worked because they were cheap enough to throw away when the joke got stale.

164. Gold and diamond PENDANT *by* LEO DE VROOMEN

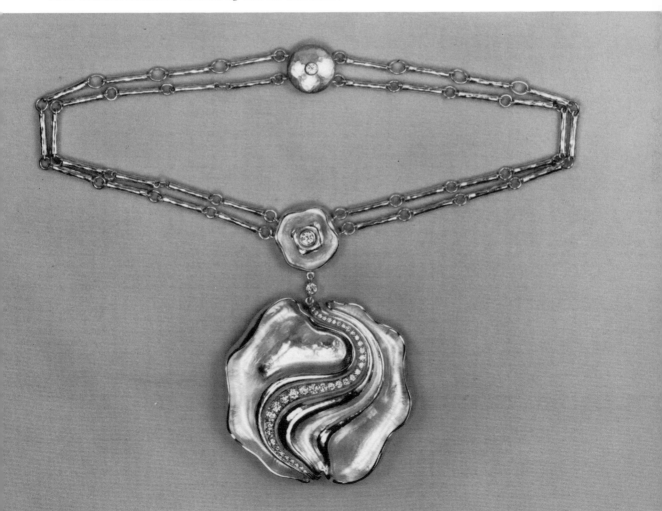

The Seventies

A little later the punk rockers of the mid-decade were wearing safety-pins in their cheeks, ears and noses; bath plugs, lavatory chains and razor blades round their necks, anti-jewels that not only affirmed their loyalties but thrust two derisive fingers up at conventional, commercial ideas of beauty and fashion.

Boys and girls alike now wear earrings, one earring for a boy if he is a straight, two if he is 'gay', and the other way about for girls. Luminous jewels made a peacetime return in the mid-seventies in the form of collars of transparent polythene tubing filled with some phosphorescent liquid. And for the first time in a civilized society jewels had to compete with the oldest and most primitive form of self-adornment as young people began to paint their faces and bodies in fantastical colours and patterns highlighted with twinkling sequins.

We have a new market now, of young people who will wear anything as long as it is out of the ordinary, does not pretend to be anything but what it is and costs less than

165. *Niobium* EARRINGS *by* LINDA ATKINSON (slightly enlarged)

thirty quid. And we have jewellers with more ideas than time to carry them out and no money to pay an assistant to do it for them. Marlene McKibbins, Caroline Broadhead and Susanna Heron quite naturally evolved styles which were economic in both labour and materials. Other jewellers like Julia Mannheim and Joel Degen began to make repeats in limited editions which the young could afford and which could be a useful way of financing more time and capital-intensive projects.

London shops like Aspect (Colour Plate XXIX) and Detail aim specifically at this market. Much of their stock is in what we are now coming to look upon as conventional materials: perspex, anodized aluminium and the refractory metals. *Linda Atkinson*, for example, works in niobium and anodized aluminium, simple basic shapes snipped out of thin sheet which allow her to ring the changes on colour and decoration and which are dazzlingly effective in wear (Plate 165).

The ingredients of other jewels in their stock are extraordinary simply because they are so commonplace: pot-scrubbers for bracelets, pink plastic pigs from a toy farm hung with imitation pearls as earrings, ping-pong balls spattered with gold paint and strung with downy feathers as a necklace. The techniques are just as wide ranging: *Gerry Roberts* makes plywood and poker-work Aztec gods; *Valerie Robertson* huge hardwood bangles gilded with squares of gold leaf; *Geoff Roberts* necklaces of leather scraps and brass foil whiskered with thongs.

It is tempting to look for similarities between the Arts and Crafts movement and the best people of today. In fact, few such similarities exist, although in one sad particular little has changed and the gulf between the art schools and the trade yawns as cavernous as ever. In the years between 1895 and 1915 the Arts and Crafts people affected to despise the trade because its designs were unattractive and its working methods were impure and dishonest, charges which were largely untrue on the first count and nonsensical on the second. The trade, on the other hand, had very little time for the Arts and Crafters because their workmanship, however 'honest' and 'true', was usually inferior.

There was a brief rapprochement between trade and colleges in the sixties, but it did not seem to 'take' and the rift seems to have been widening ever since. Now the schools say that the trade is lethargic and stick-in-the-mud, and the trade says that the graduate produces designs which are impracticable—both to manufacture and to wear. There is truth in both points of view, but whatever the rights and wrongs of it the situation is a sad one—another one of those divisions which we British seem to be so good at. From the outset the art schools have been created to give the lead to industry and seldom have they succeeded in doing so. The loss is mutual because the student needs the work and the trade, whether it knows it or not, needs the ideas.

The indifference of the British trade and public has probably helped to push the more avant-garde jewellers further and further towards the fine arts, to the point where they claim that what they are making is not jewellery at all and that only incidentally should it be worn upon the person. If it is not jewellery then clearly we must find another word for it: body sculpture has been suggested but does not always seem appropriate.

Established ideas have been excitingly and dangerously challenged. It was once

166. Acrylic and elastic BRACELET *by* SARAH McHUGH

thought that jewels should lie snugly and comfortably on the body without hampering the movements or entangling the clothing. Now some say that jewels are designed to challenge and question, to make the lady move in a way in which she would not otherwise move, to sit in a way in which she would not otherwise sit and to discover herself in the process: an interesting echo of the medieval ascetic idea of mortifying the flesh to gain inner wisdom.

Reduced to its crudest terms, the idea is that here is a piece of miniature sculpture and if somebody wants to wear it that is up to them—it is a work of art first and an object of personal adornment second. The fact is that there are more buyers for jewellery than there are for works of art—rough pragmatism but people do have to eat and in these days of economic depression young jewellers need all the friends they can find. The danger is that the buying public will flirt with these ideas and ultimately reject them. When that happens it could be that much that is good will be thrown away at the same time. The whole modern jewellery movement could be injured by it: one has only to recall the speed and savagery with which fashion turned upon art nouveau in the early 1900s.

Today's more brilliant people will adapt and survive, but what about the others only slightly less talented who have nailed their colours to this particular masthead. And it would be sad indeed if instruction in jewellery-making were ever again reduced to the level at which it stood between the wars. Despite all this, these experiments are enormously enriching and nothing worth while is ever gained without a certain amount of danger.

The fact is that the Arts and Crafts movement had more to do with political theorizing and social experimenting than with the business of making jewellery well and this was one of the reasons for its downfall. Today's jewellers are committed to technical as well as aesthetic excellence, with making the perfect piece. Some may have scruples about using ivory or diamonds for idealistic reasons, but this is as far as their personal beliefs are allowed to impinge on their work, and for the majority the creative process is in itself so all absorbing that there is no room for any other philosophy.

Bibliography

Ashbee, C. R., *Craftsmanship in Competitive Industry*, Campden, 1908

Beaumont-Nesbit, B., *Synthetic Jewellery*, catalogue of a touring exhibition compiled by East Midlands Arts, . . .

Beaumont-Nesbit, B., *The Observer Jewellery Exhibition*, catalogue of an exhibition compiled by the Welsh Arts Council, 1973

Becker, Vivienne, *Antique and Twentieth Century Jewellery*, London, 1980

Birmingham City Museum and Art Gallery, *Arthur and Georgina Gaskin*, catalogue of an exhibition

Blakemore, K., *The Retail Jewellers Guide*, London, 1976

Bradford, Ernle, *Contemporary Jewellery and Silver Design*, London, 1950

Bury, Shirley, 'New Light on the Liberty Metalwork Venture', *Decorative Arts Society Bulletin*

Cartlidge, Barbara, *The Ring from Antiquity to the Twentieth Century*, London, 1981

Clark, Hilary, *Mineral Jewellery*, catalogue of a touring exhibition compiled by East Midlands Arts, 1977

Dresser, C., *The Art of Decorative Design*, London, 1862

Edwards, R., *The Technique of Jewellery*, London, 1977

Fine Art Society, *Jewellery and Jewellery Design and John Paul Cooper 1869–1933*, catalogue of an exhibition, London, 1975

Flower, Margaret, *Victorian Jewellery*, London, 1967

Gere, Charlotte, *European and American Jewellery*, London, 1975

Gere, Charlotte, *Victorian Jewellery Design*, London, 1972

Hoskins, Sarah, and Dawson, Jan, *Organic Jewellery*, catalogue of a touring exhibition compiled by Leicester Museum and East Midlands Arts, 1975

Houston, J., *The Craftsman's Art*, Victoria and Albert Museum catalogue, London, 1973

Hughes, G., *Modern Jewellery 1890–1967*, London, 1968

Lucie Smith, E., *World of the Makers*, London, 1975

McCarthy, Fiona, *The Simple Life of C.R. Ashbee in the Cotswolds*, London, 1981

Mourey, G., *Art Nouveau Jewellery and Fans*, London, 1900; reprinted as *Art Nouveau Jewellery and Fans*, London, 1973

Munn, G., 'The Giuliano Family, Art Jewellers', *Connoisseur*, June, 1975

Munn, G., 'The Garden of Earthly Delights', *Connoisseur*, June, 1979

Turner, R., *Contempory Jewellery*, London, 1976

Turner, R., *On Tour: Ten British Jewellers in Germany—Austria*, Crafts Advisory Council and British Council, London, 1975

Victoria and Albert Museum, *Gerda Flockinger and Sam Herman Glass*, catalogue of an exhibition, London, 1971

Victoria and Albert Museum, *Liberty's 1875–1975*, catalogue of a centenary exhibition, London, 1975

Victoria and Albert Museum, *Wendy Ramshaw*, catalogue of an exhibition, London, 1982

Wilson, H., *Silverwork and Jewellery*, reprinted, London, 1948

Worshipful Company of Goldsmiths, *International Exhibition of Modern Jewellery, 1890–1961*, catalogue, London, 1961

Worshipful Company of Goldsmiths, *Loot Exhibition Catalogues*, 1975–1981

Worshipful Company of Goldsmiths, *Explosion: Talent Today*, London, 1977

Index

Index

Index